**Float like a Butterfly,
Drink Mint Tea**

FLOAT LIKE A BUTTERFLY, DRINK MINT TEA

How I Beat the Shit Out of All My Addictions

ALEX WOOD

ROBIN'S EGG BOOKS
AN IMPRINT OF
ARSENAL PULP PRESS
VANCOUVER

ROBIN'S EGG BOOKS is an imprint of
ARSENAL PULP PRESS
Suite 202 – 211 East Georgia St.
Vancouver, BC V6A 1Z6
Canada
arsenalpulp.com

The publisher gratefully acknowledges the support of the Canada Council for the Arts and the British Columbia Arts Council for its publishing program, and the Government of Canada, and the Government of British Columbia (through the Book Publishing Tax Credit Program), for its publishing activities.

Arsenal Pulp Press acknowledges the xʷməθkʷəy̓əm (Musqueam), Sḵwx̱wú7mesh (Squamish), and səl̓ilwətaʔɬ (Tsleil-Waututh) Nations, custodians of the traditional, ancestral, and unceded territories where our office is located. We pay respect to their histories, traditions, and continuous living cultures and commit to accountability, respectful relations, and friendship.

Cover and text design by Jazmin Welch
Edited by Charles Demers
Copy edited by Shirarose Wilensky
Proofread by Alison Strobel

Printed and bound in Canada

Library and Archives Canada Cataloguing in Publication:
Title: Float like a butterfly, drink mint tea : how I beat the shit out of all my addictions /
    Alex Wood.
Other titles: How I beat the shit out of all my addictions
Names: Wood, Alex, 1986– author.
Identifiers: Canadiana (print) 20200322966 | Canadiana (ebook) 2020032313X |
    ISBN 9781551528335 (softcover) | ISBN 9781551528342 (HTML)
Subjects: LCSH: Wood, Alex, 1986-—Alcohol use. | LCSH: Wood, Alex, 1986-—Drug use. |
    LCSH: Recovering addicts—Canada—Biography. | LCSH: Compulsive behavior. |
    LCGFT: Autobiographies.
Classification: LCC HV5805.W66 A3 2021 | DDC 362.29/092—dc23

For Ali and Otis

contents

foreword by charles demers   9

prologue: the fight of my life   13

PART 1: Cocaine

chapter 1: i shook up the world   23

chapter 2: miley   39

PART 2: Alcohol

chapter 3: withdrawal   61

chapter 4: playing the tape out   81

chapter 5: two fighters   95

chapter 6: wish you were here   109

PART 3: Alex Wood Quits Everything

chapter 7: april fool   **117**

chapter 8: weed   **121**

chapter 9: caffeine   **131**

chapter 10: nail biting   **159**

chapter 11: cigarettes   **167**

chapter 12: red meat   **185**

chapter 13: dairy   **189**

chapter 14: porn   **199**

chapter 15: credit cards   **209**

chapter 16: gossip   **213**

chapter 17: sugar   **221**

chapter 18: social media   **227**

chapter 19: smartphone   **241**

epilogue: the fight of my life   **257**

acknowledgments   **269**

foreword

In the summer of 2009, Alex Wood, author of the handsome volume you hold in your hands right now, and I, its handsome editor, competed against each other in the same comedy competition at the Just for Laughs comedy festival held, that year, in both Toronto and Montreal. You will read, in these pages, about how Alex's experiences at the festival were shaped by the demons of his addictions to drugs and alcohol. But what I can also tell you is that, at one of the shows we did together that week, I had a ball of toilet paper jammed between my bum cheeks, and that fact is not unrelated to my own struggle with addiction.

Earlier that day, my wife, Cara, had joined me for a walk up Montreal's Rue Saint-Denis, before her flight back to Vancouver, and along the walk I'd shared the feelings of inadequacy and insecurity that being at the festival (a childhood dream, as it had been for Alex) had brought up for me, as well as my worries that I couldn't properly enjoy the festival because of a looming book deadline (for evil and unforgiving publishers Arsenal Pulp Press—google them, or look at the copyright page of this book). So when we happened upon a candy shop, I decided to soothe my pain the way I so often had: with a large bag of gummy candies.

It wasn't always gummy candies. Sometimes it was the large cardboard flats of bags of chips my grandmother had in her basement, which I would empty in such a way that I could convince myself she couldn't tell I was eating them. Or the doughnuts I'd wait until a minute after midnight to buy, and eat, by the dozen with my friends as a teenager so that they'd be available at day-old prices. Or the platter of birthday ribs a friend of my father's made for me that I ate until I threw up. And so often, after I'd throw up from overeating, I would think to myself: *You know what that means there's room for again?* In the years after my mother (the Robin for whom this imprint is named) died when I was ten, I simply lost the ability to be sated.

Still—why did I shove toilet paper up my ass?

That afternoon in Montreal, I'd found one of those loopholes in the moral universe that the compulsive eater dreams about, like Diet Coke, or an elderly relative from whom it would be rude to resist a seventh helping: the bag of gummy candies was sugar-free! I could eat as many as I wanted, as I *needed*, without worrying about the consequences. Until an hour or two later, when I nearly shat myself in a shopping mall.

As it happens, the gummies had been sweetened with the kind of sugar alcohols that, on a package of, say, sugar-free Werther's Originals, would come with a warning not to overindulge. However, no such warning appears when one is buying in bulk. Despite drinking an entire bottle of Pepto-Bismol (something not even recommended in the Pepto-Bismol subreddit), my insides liquefied like the undersoil of a rural Midwestern outpost with a particularly lucrative fracking concession. Hence, the protective measures taken that night, which may go some way towards explaining the luke-warm reception I received at the comedy club. The faces of addiction are myriad; so are the assholes.

But as we go to press with this funny and heartbreaking book about addiction, written by someone you will come to know as a funny and heartbreaking addict, I am 263 days into what you could call "sober eating"—or what is called in some compulsive eating recovery circles "abstention," though I'm not doing a twelve-step program this time—which for me involves restricting the hours of the day during which I can eat. And I've been able to do that, at least in part, because of this book.

My path barely crossed with Alex's in the nine years between our Just for Laughs appearances and the publication of his *Vice* article "How to Quit Everything in 2018" in January of that year—but as soon as I read it, I knew there was a Robin's Egg Book in his story. I hope it affects you as profoundly as it did me. Even if it doesn't, it will have you laughing until you cry, and crying until you also cry. Things get pretty goddamn rough along the way, so you may want to have some tissues handy. Especially if you're sucking on some sugar-free Werther's Originals.

Charles Demers
Robin's Egg Books Editor

prologue

the fight of my life

I've been in dozens of fist fights. Growing up as a lippy kid with a lazy eye will do that. But this feels different. They're going to call me for my walk to the ring any second. I'm bouncing nervously in place throwing some hapless jabs. I can deal with the nerves though. I'm a stand-up comedian and it goes with the territory. Two months ago I was even a guest on NBC's *Today Show* with 3 millions people watching. But this feels different. I've been in fights I knew I was going to win; those were easy. There are other fights that aren't so easy, and even though you're not supposed to let the doubt creep in, you know in your heart, you could lose. This feels just like that.

Standing beside me is my six-one, 170-pound, tattooed Australian opponent. I've seen him train; I know he's a better boxer than me. He looks calm. I start bouncing up and down again, and I knock over a couple of empty beer kegs that I didn't know were beside me. The loud crash attracts the eyes of the other boxers and trainers backstage. I couldn't seem more like I was having my first fight if I was yelling, "Does the bell mean stop or go? I'm confused!" This stoic Aussie looks like his arms and body are growing longer by the second right in front of me. There's already a fight going on in my head between positive thoughts and negative ones.

Just like we trained, be there first.

How does this guy only weigh 170 pounds?

Cut off the ring and bring the fight to him.

I should have just run a marathon instead. I don't know the exact rules of a marathon, but I'm fairly certain you don't usually get knocked out.

There's no way I'm losing.

I drank too much water. If he punches me in the gut, I'm going to piss all over both of us. Is that a disqualification?

The ring announcer breaks my train of thought. "And now our first fighter of the evening, from Sault Ste. Marie ..."

That's my cue.

• • •

"Alex Wood?" The emergency room attendant calls my name.

It's two and half years earlier. I'm drenched in sweat, there's vomit on my shirt, and I'm shaking uncontrollably, but I manage to heave myself from my chair and walk across the room. As I'm making my way, a man in a wheelchair wheels himself to the middle of the ER, yells out, "I've got an announcement to make," and then stands up. In my delirious state I think I've just witnessed a miracle. This man is about to speak the words I've needed to hear my entire life but didn't know until this very moment.

"Don't kill Jesus."

Um, maybe?

"Kill his father."

Nope.

My mother and I are waiting for the doctor, and she insists that because of my condition she should advocate on my behalf.

"Fine, Mom. But I swear to God, if you say one embarrassing thing, I'm taking over."

"That's fine, honey."

A few minutes later the doctor enters. "What seems to be the problem?" he says.

"Well, first of all, he's very scared right now and—"

"That's enough, Mom."

"Honey, I just want the doctor to know—"

"That's enough, Mom," I say more sternly. I'm an adult now. I haven't been her little baby boy, dependent on her for everything, since I was twenty-five.

I tell the doctor everything about the last few days. About the shaking, the sweating, the nausea, the tremors, the loss of balance, and the insomnia.

"Do you drink?" the doctor asks.

Normally, I have this lie rehearsed for when a doctor asks. *Maybe a glass of white wine at book club if we're getting crazy.* But this time I feel like I'm dying, so I know I have to be truthful.

"Yes, I drink."

"How many drinks a week?"

"Eighty. Maybe more. I don't know. Who counts?"

"Eighty or more? When is the last time you had a drink?"

"Two days ago."

"And then the shaking started?"

"Yes. Well, no. That's when it got really bad, but I've had them for a bit."

"Any medical conditions?"

"Pancreatitis."

"These symptoms are alcohol withdrawal. You should seek treatment. It sounds like you're maybe an alcoholic."

"I'm not an alcoholic."

"How do you know?"

"'Cause I've gone on three-month benders where I was blind stinking drunk every night and I didn't get withdrawal symptoms when they stopped."

"Did you just tell me you got drunk every night for three months in a row as proof you're not an alcoholic?"

After that line, the doctor drops a mic and falls backwards into his group of screaming hype men and nurses. After he verbally checkmated me, the doctor gave me some benzos and a prescription for more. If you don't know what benzos are, you better get a lot hipper a lot quicker cause we are going to be covering nearly every drug known to man in this book. Benzodiazepine is a tranquilizer that is prescribed for severe alcohol withdrawal symptoms. I was given a warning not to abuse the benzos because they are addictive. I was a bank robber the cops had just busted but then given a new gun and ski mask on the honour system.

Twenty minutes after I take the benzos, the shaking and the sweating subside, and I fall asleep to the beeping of medical equipment.

The darkness is interrupted by a blood-curdling scream.

"Fire in the hole!" Captain Dunn cries.

It's seventy-five years earlier. The ringing in my ears stops minutes later. I scan the once-beautiful French beach, now wearing the hallmarks of war. Bodies lie scattered like the carcasses of wild animals, and the normally blue tide is now red. Whatever innocence was left in my soul has been taken this day—

Whoops, I went too far back and into a past life with that last flashback. I'll try to stay more focused.

Here's the deal: I'm an addict and I always have been. I've been leaving places because I couldn't handle my shit since I was a child. At birthday parties I would have pizza and orange pop until I threw up. No one recognizes addict behaviour in kids. It's not like the other eight-year-olds were saying to each other, "I'm worried about Alex's orange pop consumption. Last week I saw him puke on the monkey bars." In my life I've also thrown up in/on: a beer glass; a pitcher; a urinal; a bank machine; a bench; myself; my bed; a car; a bus; a van; an airplane; an airport; a train; a boat; several different people, most of whom I'm not currently on speaking terms with; and a raccoon. Not all of those times were from orange pop.

I'm the middle child. I have an older brother, Zac, and a younger sister, Kate. They're successful, wonderful people, and although I love them, I will openly admit to my favourite sibling being Bob. An eighty-five-pound chow-collie rescue who was the dog prince of the family. When we ordered pizza Bob got a slice and most of the crusts. Bob had suffered abuse in his previous home. Making him happy made me happy, and when I was happy it made him happy. We had a perfect symbiotic relationship. Bob was the only living thing I ever fully trusted, except with my food when I wasn't in the room. A lot of the things I'm going to tell you in this book I told Bob before anyone else. It pains me that I can't devote more time to him, but my editor already reprimanded me for my first draft being mostly a retelling of the film *Top Gun* starring Bob and me.

My mom and dad split up when I was six, and my mom took us kids from our hometown to live in Ottawa. We would spend the summers with my father and the school year with my mother.

My dad was like two guys in the same person. The first guy always seemed to be able to make people around him feel comfortable. A supportive, loving man who would break his back all day in a paper mill just so he could get me tickets to the see the Toronto Maple Leafs play in Montreal against the Canadiens for *Hockey Night in Canada*. He would tell me that I had to help people who are weaker than me because it was my responsibility. He was generous and gregarious. Hopeful and fun. Inspired and inspiring. Most of the time. I loved that guy.

The other guy was an angry asshole that I would have fought if I weren't so terrified of him. That guy would grab me by the neck and throw me across the room when he was angry. He would tell me that I was a fuck-up because I didn't shovel the driveway to his liking. As I got older, it felt like the first guy was increasingly slipping away every year and the second guy was around more and more. He was hurtful and humiliating. Scared and scary. I hated that guy.

My mom is the toughest person I have ever met. A lot of kids like to say, "My dad could beat up your dad." Well, my mom could kick the living shit out of your dad. When I was a kid, she worked for customs at the border between the twin Sault Ste. Maries of Canada and the States. For someone whose job it was to catch people with drugs, she sure wasn't good at catching me with them. After we moved to Ottawa, as a single mother of three, she went back to school at night and got a job working for Revenue Canada. She was tireless and strong. Unwavering and unstoppable. Even after she got sick. She was diagnosed with multiple sclerosis when I was fourteen. It started with shaking, but then she started having trouble walking. Eventually, she started taking some pretty bad falls. My mom may fall down sometimes, but she never stays down. I thought she could do anything. Except quit smoking, but we'll get to that.

I'm not famous, and I know the childhood part of even a famous person's story is boring—"Yeah, yeah, working-class Liverpool and all that. Get to the Beatles already." Although my childhood, and the trauma that came with it, led me to what this book is really about, it's not what this book is about, even if it is kind of what this book is about. It's confusing, I know. Welcome to being an addict.

This is a story about fighting with the past, battling addiction, falling in love, losing yourself, finding yourself, and the comedy in between. Oh, and boxing. And remembering the people you love who aren't here anymore. I guess it's a little bit about the modern world's hold on people with technology. And the real-life sexual repercussions of watching pornography. Actually, there's a decent amount about dogs in here, too. It's a story about a lot of things, okay?

But mostly this is a story about how, in a three-year period, from February 2015 to April 2018, I quit: cocaine, alcohol, weed, caffeine, nail biting, cigarettes, red meat, dairy, porn, credit cards, gossip, sugar, social media, and my smartphone.

We're going to engage in some time travelling, too, because to understand the present you must know the past. I've also always wanted to write a novel about a dystopian future, and since I'm the one writing this book, that very well might happen. I've got five words for you: Cyborg Hulk Hogan: World President. Along the way I'll hide some things from you because that's what addicts do, but otherwise, I make this solemn pledge to you, dear reader, I will be unflinchingly and uncompromisingly honest.

Enough preamble—let us begin at the base of Everest, where I am about to become the first person to moonwalk up the world's tallest mountain! Oh, right, that whole honesty thing. Okay, then I guess let's start at the strip club in Montreal where I just relapsed on cocaine.

PART 1

Cocaine

chapter 1

i shook up the world

It's Valentine's Day 2015, and I can feel my heart beating faster as the euphoria washes over me. Only two things can give me such intense feelings: love and cocaine. And I love cocaine. The problems start, like they do tonight, when the bag is empty and all I want is more. Even though it's not a secret that a strip club is a good place to find cocaine, you're supposed to be stealthy about it. Not go to every table like a little kid selling chocolate bars door to door, like I am. Except instead of trying to sell cocoa, I'm trying to buy coca. The bouncers don't seem pleased with my raving lunatic approach to trying to score, so they escort me out of the building. They switch from escorting to dragging when I beg them to help me get blow.

This isn't the last time we'll visit a strip club in this story, not even close. Actually, I almost called this book *No Champagne in the Sex Room: My Life in Strip Clubs and Sobriety*.

Before that night it had been almost two years since the last time I did coke. I could never seem to go longer than two years without it. The first time I tried cocaine I was seventeen. They say not to marry young, but I would have said my vows right then and there:

I, Alex, take you, cocaine, to be my unlawfully wedded wife. To have and to snort, from this day forward, for better or for much worse, for poor or for poorer, in sickness and in poor mental health until my death do us part. You may now lick the bottom of the bag.

All of my anxiety, fear, distrust, hurt, and pain—gone. It went away, or at least it felt like it did. I didn't need anyone to love me, or to love myself. I just needed more of this. A lot more.

That first morning after doing cocaine I had a hangover unlike any other before it. I'd had some nasty ones by this point, too, because I'd been binge drinking until I passed out since I was fourteen. It wasn't sadness, it wasn't regret, and it certainly wasn't happiness. It was nothingness. Emptiness. Going forward, I wish I had remembered the feeling the morning after instead of the one the night before. The nothingness didn't occur to me the next weekend when I did cocaine again. And it didn't occur to me when I did cocaine almost every weekend for the next six months. The first time I did a gram of cocaine in one night, by myself, I had to sleep without shutting off the lights. My heart was beating so hard and so fast that I thought I should keep a light on. *In case I'm close to dying in my sleep*, my thinking went, *maybe the light will keep me alive*. My life was sex, drugs, and rock 'n' roll, baby! Okay, I did promise honesty. I had no musical ability and was still a virgin.

I started doing something else around that time, too. I'd had a few dream jobs in mind when I was a kid. By the time I was ten, enough shots had fired from the other team's end, past my lazy eye, and into the net behind me for me to figure out I wouldn't make it as an NHL goalie. There was another dream I accepted was out of my reach. "Idolized" isn't the word for how I felt about boxers; "deified" would be more appropriate, from the giants of the past like Frazier, Foreman, Durán, Robinson, and Hagler to the stars of my childhood like De La Hoya, Jones Jr., Hopkins, Gatti, and Lewis. One boxer always stood out as my favourite, even though he'd retired before I was born. I would watch the old fights, the documentaries, and the interviews. I went to Catholic school for fourteen years, but the only thing I could quote like scripture was Muhammad Ali. I promised myself that one day I would get a "Rumble, young man, rumble" tattoo. But even though I had been in plenty of fights, I knew in my heart I could never be a boxer. I thought boxers weren't scared of anything, and I was scared of plenty. I reasoned that a boxer would never have let what happened to me happen to them. So I turned to my backup plan: professional funny person. I *knew* they're fucked up.

I always tried to make every event into my own comedy performance. School, family dinners, major holidays, weddings, birthday parties—they were all just shows for me. I found out at an early age that school wasn't for me. I considered my real education to be what happened after the final bell, when I would go home to watch the Canadian institution *Just for Laughs* on television every day instead of doing my homework. For my grade six talent show I performed jokes that I shamelessly stole from my favourite comic: Mike MacDonald. If I couldn't be starting goalie for the Toronto Maple Leafs or heavyweight champion of the world, comedian was my dream job.

I was eighteen when I signed up for amateur night at Yuk Yuk's Comedy Club in Ottawa, the same club where Mike MacDonald got his start. That's the best part about comedy. If you want to be a boxer, you spend hundreds of hours training before your first fight. If you want to be a comedian, your first fight is the first night you ever walk onto a stage. No practice. It's as if your debut bout is the first time you ever put gloves on and Sugar Shane Mosley is across the ring from you. I was scared that I wouldn't be good. I was scared that I was just the funniest in my school, not funny enough to be a comedian. But I had to know. I kept it a secret because I thought there was a good chance I would fail miserably and instantly quit. I would have nothing to show for it but a bar story about "the time I tried stand-up comedy." A word to the wise, if you ever meet someone who tries to tell you the story about the time they tried stand-up comedy, call in a bomb threat to whatever place you happen to be in, or if you're fortunate enough to have a working bomb with you, detonate it.

My family went over to my uncle Noel's house for dinner that night (you'll meet him again later). I couldn't even eat I was so nervous. I excused myself from the table and started pacing in the living room.

My mom walked in. "You're going to Yuk Yuk's to do comedy tonight, aren't you?"

It was the connection my mom and I have always had. Not only did she somehow just know, but also I wasn't even surprised that she did.

"Yes, Mom. I'm so nervous. I was confident all day, but the show starts in an hour and I am freaking out. I don't know if I can do this."

"You were meant to do this."

I got to the club for amateur night expecting a red carpet to be laid out in front of me with a banner reading, *Welcome, New Comedic Genius*. Instead, I didn't even get a hello. I walked in and spotted my name on the list right in the middle of the show. I could see some of the comedians hanging out behind the bar, so I confidently headed over to join them, before the bartender told me that no one was allowed behind the bar. And that's pretty much all you need to know about what it's like starting out in comedy. Seeing six people standing right in front of you behind a line while someone tells you that no one is allowed past the line.

I watched a few people bomb pretty hard. I was like a man on death row awaiting his fate, except that when the priest asks if he has any final words, he says, "Anyone here from out of town?" I did jokes about the savage beatings my older brother used to lay on me, and my masturbation habits, as well as one bit about heaven probably getting boring if it truly is for eternity. "Even meeting God enough times would lose its magic. I imagine that by the tenth time God would just be like that annoying co-worker that's always talking about his son and you have to pretend to be interested. 'Wow, how old is he now? Two thousand years old! They grow up so fast. Five thousand people with only one loaf of bread? Ya don't say.'"

I didn't kill. I didn't bomb. I got a few decent laughs and one big one. When I got off the stage the surly club manager, Howard, told me, "You weren't scared up there. It was all right." I was only eighteen when I started as a comedian, and it's the only thing I've ever been good at right away. It gave me feelings of hope, purpose, confidence, ambition, and control that I'd never had before. It did something else, too. Getting fucked up made me feel like I had a place to hide. Comedy made me feel like maybe one day I wouldn't have to.

Usually, I outright reject guidance of any kind, but when it was coming from Jocko I tried to listen. Jocko was bold, bald, biracial, half French, charismatic, and silky smooth onstage. He was large in stature and structure. Jocko loved the simple things in life: comedy, sports, Elvis, and his new baby girl, appropriately named Presley. Jocko always killed. I mean, always. He was automatic. He was like a machine sent back in time by robots and programmed to do one thing and one thing alone: kill audiences. As we would drive through whiteout conditions to bars in far-flung towns he would tell me about comedy being a business, about the work that goes into it offstage, and about what makes a professional comedian. When we weren't talking about that, we'd talk about life, and about Ali. I listened to all the things Jocko ever told me, except one. Jocko always used to say that I had to quit doing drugs and drinking all the time. That I thought it was working for me now, but that shit doesn't last and it would catch up to me someday. The only vices we shared were greasy food and cigarettes.

My other comedy mentor was Wafik. He said I was like his comedy son and he was my comedy dad. I always thought of him as more of a brother, though, because I think you're supposed to hide the things we did together from your father. Like Jocko, Wafik also drove me to gigs—when he wasn't too drunk. He was a one-eyed Egyptian who lost sight in his left eye when another kid threw his own glasses at him. As Wafik says, "Sometimes you don't pick comedy; comedy picks you." His TV special had just come out when we met, and he was the undisputed champ of the Ottawa comedy scene. We had so much in common: strict fathers, little-to-no vision out of our left eyes, and the same mortal enemy: ourselves. Wafik was the only person I knew who smoked as much weed and drank as much as I did. We also did a lot of blow together. He had great advice about where to go to score drugs in any city in Canada that had a comedy club. Like Jocko, Wafik had a daughter, but he didn't get to see her much because of custody battles. Jocko would give me shit, and Wafik would give me cocaine. I listened to one of my comedy teachers way more than the other—take a guess which one.

But it's a good thing I had them, and my uncle Noel, because I had pretty much stopped speaking to my father by then. The final straw was when I had to go back to Sault Ste. Marie to help him move into a new house.

I took the twelve-hour Greyhound bus ride back to my hometown, the same Greyhound bus I had been riding to and from Sault Ste. Marie to spend summers with my father ever since my parents' divorce.

This time, as my bus pulled up at the station, I could see my dad outside. He was in a phone booth, slamming the receiver down repeatedly. I didn't even wonder. I knew what it meant. My brother was away at university, and I'd made him promise not to bail on me for this move.

"Your fucking jerk-off brother isn't here."

My brother was the favourite, so I can only imagine what my father called me behind my back.

"He was supposed to be on the bus right before you, and now he's not answering his phone. I guess it's just us. It's probably going to take us two fucking days now! Two whole fucking days!" he screamed, while smacking the car's steering wheel with his meaty hands. He hadn't even said hello yet.

The entire move was like a concert for a genre of music that can only be described as "angry dad rock." Of course he played the old favourites:

"I'm Not Asking, I'm Telling"

"Lift with Your Goddamn Legs"

"What Did I Just Say? (Hey, Asshole)"

The ballads like:

"Are You Stupid or Something?"

"Don't Give Me That Look"

And his usual encore:

"Do I Have to Fucking Smack You?"

It took all day for us to get even halfway done. Say what you will about the man's motivational tactics, but he had that move timed perfectly. Two fucking days. For a non-professional, the accuracy with which he was able to predict the length of time the move would take was pretty impressive. This was the nicest thing I had left to say about him. Things between us were getting worse with each item we moved from the truck to the house. The insults becoming harsher, deeper.

"You fucking idiot, go be a failure in your mom's basement after this for all I care."

The intense heat of the day gave way to a lightning storm, and we had one item left. A cast-iron stove, which didn't have handles. It easily weighed 300 pounds and had to be moved using only our fingers. I was surprised my dad still had any strength left after using his middle one so much.

"Can we do this one tomorrow?" I begged.

"For fuck's sake, son. Can you just do one goddamn thing without bitching?"

"It's raining and this is already so hard to move. I just don't think I can even do it."

"Stop being a fucking baby."

"I'm not moving it."

He started to walk around the stove in his classic take-two-very-angry-steps-at-me-before-I-cower-and-whimper-"okay" move.

But this time was different. I met him before he could even get around the stove and pushed him as hard as he had pushed me my entire life. I was shocked by how far back my shove forced his 280-pound frame as he landed against the wall of the moving truck with a loud thud.

"All right, you miserable fucking prick, you wanna fight me? Let's fucking fight!" I screamed louder than he had ever screamed at me.

I knew I wasn't actually ready to fight him. I was trying to shock him into realizing how maniacal he had been all day, and for so many years. I was trying to make him see that I had been pushed to my limit, and that I was his son and he was hurting me. I saw the shock in his eyes. I saw the father who told me after I let in eight goals in one game that he was proud of me because I never quit. I saw the father who held my siblings and me so tight when he told us he loved us.

But as quickly as I saw that father, I saw the other guy take over. His eyes changed again. "Take off your glasses," he said.

I screamed even louder now. So loud my voice box hurt. "What the fuck is wrong with you? I'm your fucking son and you're ready to fucking fight me!"

"Move this fucking stove and we never have to see each other again," he said.

That was all the motivation I needed. I moved that stove in the hot rain, hoping a bolt of lightning would hit it while we were holding it and kill one or both of us.

The next day was more of the same. The day after that, he dropped me off at the Greyhound station. I had one thought running through my brain the entire twelve-hour ride home.

I'm not even going to your funeral.

• • •

Over the next couple of years I wasn't good at much other than getting fucked up, eating a smorgasbord of terrible food, and doing comedy. So I poured myself into all three. My weight ballooned to 240 pounds, and I smoked weed all day, drank all night, and did cocaine any chance I got.

But something good also happened. Less than four years into doing comedy, when I was only twenty-two years old, I was selected to perform at the Just for Laughs festival in the Homegrown show, an annual competition of rising Canadian stand-up talent from across the country. It's not televised, but it's the stepping stone to a TV taping. I had two months before the show to get ready, and I knew I had to clean up for it. Jocko and I planned out what jokes I would tell and even what I would wear. I cut back on my drinking significantly—I was down to twenty drinks a week. And I stopped doing cocaine entirely.

I was beginning to think maybe I shouldn't be doing it that often anyway. It was every weekend for a year at this point. There were other subtle signs of possible dependence. Like how I would lick whatever object I had done it off of afterwards. That quickly turned into licking whatever surface was underneath the object I had just done it off of (an act so vile I nearly called this book *Bad Habits and Hairballs: How I Got Rug Burns on My Tongue*). Hardwood floor is one thing, but when you're licking the carpet in your bedroom at six a.m. things should start clicking that maybe you don't have a handle on this.

I was still smoking weed every day, but I didn't do it all day. I even tried to limit my cigarette smoking because I was starting to feel like it was hurting my onstage stamina. I treated the two months before the show like a boxing training camp. All right, it's not like there are deleted scenes in the Rocky movies where he cuts back to half a pack a day between bong hits and whiskeys. This was my own version—*Rocky VI: Lazy Eye of the Tiger*.

That year, for the first time, the festival was taking place in both Toronto and Montreal. I would have one show in Toronto, which would be the contest part of Homegrown, and two in Montreal—including one at a theatre with an audience of 400, which would be double the size of the biggest crowd I had performed in front of to that point. I had a decent set in Toronto. I was nervous off the top, but by the middle I was popping the crowd big time. However, on a lineup of merciless killers, my set was forgettable. I didn't win, but I was okay with it. I just wanted to kill the theatre show in Montreal the way I had dreamed of since I was a kid. My resolve to restrain myself had worn off, though, and I got recently-divorced-man drunk every night for the entire week in Montreal.

The first night in *la belle province* I was waiting for the doors to open outside a venue in the pouring rain, trying to light a damp joint to no avail. And that's when I saw Mike MacDonald in real life for the first time. He walked out of the shadows holding an umbrella and seemed as large a figure to me as he had been on TV. I no longer cared about the rain stopping me from lighting my joint as it dangled from my lips. The man whose jokes I had stolen for my grade six talent show was unmistakably coming towards me. What could he possibly want with me?

"Looks like we both have something that the other could use," he said, as he put the umbrella over my head and looked down at the joint in my mouth.

I lit it and passed it to the man I was in awe of.

"You know, this is really cool for me because when I was in grade six I did one of your *Just for Laughs* sets for my class talent show."

Mike took a deep pull from the joint. As the smoke billowed out of his mouth he said, "Sounds like you owe me a cut of what you made on the gig."

We ended up watching the show together. Afterwards, he turned to me and said, "Is this your first time at the festival?"

"Yes, it is."

"I'm going to give you a piece of advice."

Whatever he says I am taking like a papal bull.

"Don't be the last one to leave the bar. Have a good show, kid."

The Babe Ruth of Canadian comedy disappeared into the night the same way he'd appeared, and I was convinced of two things: it would be the last time I saw him, and I wouldn't be the last one to leave the bar ever again.

Two days later, at six a.m., I was the last one to leave the bar at the Hyatt. Sorry, Mike, the drinks were free. What was I supposed to do? The biggest show of my life—no, the biggest moment of my life—was in thirteen hours and I was hammered. I got back to my hotel room and collapsed in my bed wearing the same clothes I'd had on all week.

I woke up to my hotel room phone ringing. "Hey, just want to let you know the shuttle is going to pick you up in fifteen minutes to go to the gig."

I hopped in the shower, praying to the god I didn't believe in that he would instantly rid me of this hangover.

He did not. I got to the lobby and the other comedians on the show looked refreshed and excited. I was just hoping I wouldn't puke onstage. My pre-show joint helped with the nausea but not the nerves.

When I got backstage I discovered that I was on third. Not enough time to recuperate. Why didn't I listen to Mike? Why don't I ever listen? I watched in horror as the host and the first two acts struggled to open up the crowd. They were so tight no one was getting decent laughs. I accepted my fate to bomb. I don't know what came over me, but during the act before mine, I started to dance. I figured if I was going to bomb the biggest show of my life while nursing a brutal hangover, I was going to have fun doing it.

Five minutes later, I heard the emcee say my name.

I grabbed the microphone and began. "I saw a sign in the grocery store that said, *Lost Dog: Partially Blind and Deaf*. I wanted to be a good citizen, so I called the number and said, 'Hi, I just saw your sign. I just wanted to let you know, that dog is fucking dead.'"

I could feel the vibrations from how hard the crowd erupted with laughter. And I felt those same vibrations more times throughout my set. I didn't kill; I slaughtered. It remains, to this day, the best six-minute set I've ever had.

Every year there is a legendary ball hockey game played between the comedians and the employees of the festival called the Artists versus Industry Game. It took place the morning after my show and the twelve-hour celebration that followed. I'd had my last drink at nine a.m., and the game started at eleven. The artists won the game and the trophy that went with it. My final stat line was zero goals, zero assists, and three puking fits into the garbage can on the bench. It always bugs me when I see Michael Jordan's flu game mentioned as one of the greatest sports performances and not mine. It's all politics.

There were open bars, after-parties, after-after-parties, strip clubs, and free pizza. Any combination of those words is enough for me, but it got better. I got to crack jokes with some of the biggest comedians in the world. I was making people laugh that I had been quoting since I was in high school. When the festival ended I returned home with a copy of the *Montreal Gazette* that had an article titled "Best of the Fest" that featured me and one of my jokes.

Muhammad Ali beat Sonny Liston in one of the all-time biggest sports upsets to capture his first world title when he was only twenty-two. He was in hysterics in the ring afterwards, screaming over and over again, "I shook up the world! I shook up the world!"

I was twenty-two in Montreal, and I know my set didn't shake up the world. But it shook up my world.

I always felt like a terrified child just playing an adult in a school play. Any minute my fake moustache would fall off and I would be exposed. But after Just for Laughs I finally felt like I wasn't just a scared little boy anymore.

chapter 2

miley

You see, I do this thing, when things are going well, where I kind of, sort of, fuck it all up. But I wasn't going to do that this time.

I'm feeling more motivated than ever to go after my dreams. I'm going to get a day job and save some money so I can move to Toronto to really pursue comedy. I'm going to start writing new jokes, sketches, pilots, and screenplays. I have some industry recognition now, and this is my time. I'm just going to do some coke tonight because I haven't in a while. I just got back from the festival; I deserve it, and then it's right down to business. More like write down to business. God, that's a great pun. That's enough work for today; let's blow off some steam. Another fantastic pun. I'm killing this already and it's only been a week since Just for Laughs ended. Let's grab some more coke and keep this party going. All right, that was fun, but now it's time to get to work; I have a lot of shows this week. Although I wonder what it would be like to do a set on coke. That was electric! If performing on cocaine is like that, what would writing on it be like? Genius incarnate! I wrote thirty pages in one day. I don't even need to read them; I know that was good shit. Speaking of good shit, I could use some more coke. September already? Fuck. I guess doing cocaine alone during the daytime can really let the calendar get away from you.

I better stop doing it for a bit. I'll just do it this one last time before I stop for a while. Okay, no, this one last time. Whoa, today really sucks; I'm desperate for some. I can't even remember the last day I didn't do any cocaine. Middle of August maybe? That's like—wait, what's today? Almost October. Have I done cocaine every day for six weeks? No, that can't be right. Maybe it is; I'm not sure. Do I have a problem? No, I just got carried away. Let's stop doing cocaine for a long while. But a proper goodbye is in order first.

There are a lot of reasons I did cocaine heavily almost every single day and drank heavily every single day from the end of Just for Laughs in July until the end of my rope in October. It was ninety days of being completely and utterly, beyond-repair, fall-down, teeth-clenching, liver-hurting, brain-damaging fucked up. I spent everything I had made on drugs and booze and still managed to ring up a $2,200 cocaine debt. I would have a lot more benders in my life but never any quite that bad. Everyone was telling me that I had to move to Toronto for comedy. I was given an industry push, and I had to ride that momentum. But I just couldn't. The feeling of finally being a grown-up after my set at Just for Laughs was fleeting. I was a boy again within weeks. It's a lot to ask of an alcoholic, drug-addicted, and terrified child. To move out of their mom's house and to the biggest city in the country. Another reason was that it was almost Halloween.

Usually, when the leaves fall in autumn, I do too. Most of my worst benders and relapses came during September, October, and November. All my romantic relationships had ended during those months. One time during this season, when I was eighteen, I got into a screaming match with my brother and mother. I don't even remember what started it, but I remember what ended it. Me taking a few handfuls of my mom's migraine pills. Even though it was enough to kill me, I didn't think of it as a suicide attempt. It was more of a cry for help. I had my stomach pumped at the ER that night and was forced to drink activated charcoal to prevent the pills from being absorbed into my gut. Like a lot of bad things that happened to me in my life, I never talked about it afterwards.

I guess now would be as good a time as any to tell you about this thing that follows me around. It's been there for quite some time, almost as long as I can even remember. Most of the time it's far enough away that I can breathe easy. I could live with it if it always kept a distance. But it never does for very long. No matter what I try, it always finds a way in. I can start to sense it around every corner, and the waiting is almost as bad as when it appears. Sometimes it takes weeks, moving closer inch by inch. Other times it appears out of thin air. I can't see it, though; I can only feel it.

I can always feel it in my guts before anything else. That's where it starts, ripping through my stomach, and it won't stop until I let it into the rest of my body. As much as it hurts, I try to keep it in my stomach because I know when it spreads, it hurts even more. The pain in my stomach builds and builds, until I can't hold it back any longer. It isn't long before it gets into my heart. The healthy blood my heart usually pumps into the rest of my body is now poison. Every beat sends more of the disease throughout my body. The toxins reach my brain, and that's when it has me. There's no going back once that happens. You can see my body, you might even be able to get a couple words out of me, but it's like I'm not in our world anymore; I'm in some other place.

I can only tell you this about that other place. It's so scary I would do anything to not be there. Anything. Even if it means dying.

● ● ●

It was the middle of October by the time I finally took a few days off coke, and it wasn't by choice. Wafik was on the road, my dealer cut me off because I owed him too much money, and I was flat broke. I thought I had contracted an illness because I was completely brain dead, sweating, shaking with chills, and constantly feeling like I was going to throw up. I was dope sick from withdrawal, but I thought I was just under the weather. That's how deep denial can run when you're in the throes of addiction.

I've been going really hard on the booze and coke lately. I suddenly stop and feel physically sicker than I ever have. Holy fuck. It's that swine flu (or as we call it now, the good ol' days).

It was a real bad case of the Mondays. I wasn't even able to sleep until early Tuesday morning. When I woke up, looked at my phone, and saw it was three p.m., I thought, *Wow, great—I actually slept seven hours.* Then I saw something beside the time that confused me. It was the word *Wednesday*. It took me five minutes to realize that I'd just slept for thirty-one hours.

I had a voice mail from the owner of the Absolute Comedy club in Ottawa. Jason spoke like a cocaine addict, even though he didn't do cocaine. Hundreds of words in a single minute. He was the first person to give me paid shows, spots longer than six minutes, and gigs in other cities. I was his Golden Boy. The only criticism he had for me was that I smoked too much weed. He hated cocaine, and I knew he would be furious if he found out how much I was doing in his bathroom before I would go on his stage to perform. I checked the message and it was his familiar ranting.

I promise you, this voice mail was somehow only four seconds long: "It's fucking two in the afternoon and you're still asleep, aren't you? Holy fuck, you lazy pothead, get up. I'm trying to give you money. When I was your age I never would have missed a call from a booker and cellphones weren't even a thing yet. You gotta be more professional. I need you to host the club tonight, but if you don't get back to me soon, I'll have to call someone else."

Immediately, I called him back. After all, I needed that seventy-five dollars for cocaine.

When I got to the club I didn't have that spark in my heart to perform. It may not sound like much, but that was the first time that had ever happened to me. I wasn't at the club because it's where I always thought I belonged. I wasn't there because making people laugh was the best high I ever got. I was there to make drug money.

About twenty minutes before the show I decided to try to mimic the pre-show cocaine high that I was now in full need of before going onstage. I chugged two cups of coffee and a beer, I smoked a joint and two cigarettes, and I downed a shot before grabbing another beer to take with me.

The announcer's voice said, "And now your hilarious host and emcee ..." and I started my walk to the stage with total emptiness in my heart. I put my half-empty pint glass on the stool and grabbed the mic out of the stand like I had done hundreds of times before.

"How you guys feeling tonight?"

The crowd roared with excitement.

And that's when I felt it. Something was seriously wrong. I was going to pass out.

"Your headliner is in the back of the room. Let him hear it."

The crowd roared again.

I was about to die right in front of these people. My heart was barely beating. I was dizzy. Sweat was dripping down my spine, and every muscle in my body was tensing up.

"I'll tell you guys what's going on with me—" That was just a line I would say to transition to material when I hosted. I never told anyone what was going on with me, and I wasn't about to start with these people.

"I recently—" I couldn't finish my sentence. *Oh, fuck. What is happening?* I paused.

"I recently joined a gym—" was the last thing I said before I turned to the half-empty pint glass and vomited into it. It overflowed the cup and ran down the stool and onto the stage. This was less than one minute into the show. If you haven't ever been to see stand-up comedy live, this isn't how we typically like to start a show. I've never heard a crowd that silent. It was "Is he really doing an impression of that accent right now?" silent. I'm talking "Is she really doing another ukulele song about the patriarchy?" silent.

Nick, the doorman, ran a garbage can to the stage. I wasn't even done with my hand signal to let him know that the garbage can wouldn't be necessary before I started vomiting violently into it.

The crowd's eerie silence was broken by one guy yelling out, "What the fuck?" before he was joined by horrified gasps and screams.

After I was done throwing up, the crowd went silent again. No one, least of all me, knew what they were watching. People were checking their ticket stubs like, "What kind of performance art is this?"

Nick asked me if I was going to still do the show. The microphone picked up his question and the entire crowd leaned forward in anticipation. I said yes. Nick and I always knew what the other was thinking when it came to comedy. He tossed me a softball.

"Do you need anything?"

"Maybe a ginger ale. My tummy hurts."

It's still, to this day, one of the biggest laughs I've ever gotten, onstage or off.

I told the audience that I had been fighting the flu and hadn't eaten in days, which was as close to the truth as I was telling people at that time. I then did an impression of what had just happened with a sports announcer's voice calling the action. For the next twenty minutes, people were stomping on the floor they were laughing so hard. The kitchen staff ran upstairs because they said they thought the roof was going to cave in. During the first act, Nick and I came up with another bit. I went onstage wearing a garbage bag like a poncho. I didn't even say anything, just stood there, deadpanning. Another laugh so big it actually hurt my ears. The audience comment cards at the end of the night were littered with raves like "The best thing I've ever seen" and "The hardest I've ever laughed in my life." The headliner, Andy, a veteran who had performed on *Letterman*, a comic who had seen it all, told me it was one of the most amazing things he'd ever seen onstage.

It was the last thing I needed. What should have been rock bottom was just another hero drug story: the time I was so dope sick I puked onstage and still killed. I grabbed a bag of coke that night, thankful the mysterious illness had run its course. I used the $1,200 I made from a few gigs and another $1,000 Nick loaned me to pay off my dealer. That was money I could have used to move to Toronto and capitalize on my career momentum, but I chose the drugs.

It was only two weeks later when a different fluid came out of a different hole. If you guessed I shit my pants, I'm sorry to say that my editor has demanded I remove all my anecdotes about defecating in my trousers. Which is unfortunate because I have so many of those I almost called this book *Shitting and Quitting: How I Ruined My Life and a Dozen Pairs of Jeans*.

I was back at the club, high on cocaine, hosting on a Wednesday again. As the other comedians were furiously writing their lines, I was snorting mine in the bathroom. Standing in the wings, I felt something bad happening inside of me again. *Oh fuck.* I covered my face with my hand and ran to a garbage can. A staff member cried out, "Again?"

Not quite. This time when I dropped my hand it wasn't vomit flowing freely out of me. It was blood. Lots and lots of blood. I couldn't perform. No hero story this time. Just a bloody cokehead.

The next morning I saw Jocko's number on my phone and wanted nothing to do with the call. I knew what was coming. He was gonna say, "I told you so." He would read me the riot act and tell me how stupid I was, and I just couldn't hear that right now. But five seconds after the phone stopped ringing he called me again. I figured I might as well answer.

"Yeah."

"You okay?"

"I don't think so, Jock."

"Well, you go get okay, and then come back, you hear me?"

"I hear you."

"I got your back, you hear me?"

"I hear you."

I decided I had to quit cocaine. I told everyone in the scene that I had "medical" issues I needed to figure out, and then I made a painful decision. I had to take some time away from the stage. I knew I couldn't kick this shit while doing comedy. I had to make a choice between cocaine and comedy. It would be the motivation I needed.

There was only one more step I had to take before quitting. One last fix. The timing was perfect: it was the last day of the month, it was a Saturday, and it was Halloween. I grabbed two grams of cocaine and a bottle of Jack and went to a Halloween party. Around four a.m. I looked down at what I thought would be the last line I would ever snort and said, "Goodbye" before it disappeared up my nose.

• • •

It felt like my blood was on fire the first three days off. I expected the thirty-one-hour coma-nap from the month before to happen again, but instead it was the opposite—I couldn't sleep for more than thirty minutes at a time. I was constantly aware of my heartbeat and convinced that it was off. I was soaked in sweat and constantly nauseated. All of these ailments were set to the soundtrack of random auditory hallucinations. It was like all my emotions had been turned down to zero and there was just a low hum of despair.

In the middle of the month my physical withdrawal symptoms subsided. I was sleeping my way through most days and only leaving my mom's basement to go outside for a cigarette or joint or to microwave a frozen dinner when I felt I could stomach it. It was like that first cocaine hangover when I was seventeen but lasted for weeks without an end in sight. There was nothing that could fill the emptiness. All I did was pace, plagued by one thought playing on repeat: *What if I'm like this forever?*

I started contemplating suicide. Every article I read on the internet about cocaine said it was supposed to be out of my system by now, so I didn't understand why I still couldn't see my life without it. Every morning that I woke up and didn't feel like myself brought me one step closer to killing myself. In the darkest times of my self-loathing I'd always had one thing I was proud of about being Alex Wood: I was tough enough to make it through, no matter what. But I didn't even have that anymore.

I picked a day. Six months from the last time I'd done cocaine. April 1. I'm a fool anyway, so why not? Fuck my family. Fuck my friends. Fuck comedy. Fuck everything. If I still felt like this, I would kill myself.

Then, one day, Miley Cyrus saved my life.

I woke up in the late afternoon. Another day feeling like a disappointed kid who found out Christmas didn't come this year (Christmas, for me, being not wanting to kill myself). On this day I thought that I should at least *try* to help myself. One of my favourite parts of being a comedian was my pre-show ritual. I'd throw music on the television, and then get in the shower so there would be something playing when I came out of the bathroom and I would be surprised by which song it was. It always put me in a good mood and made me ready to perform. Music had been nothing but cacophony for me since I went cold turkey hundreds of years (or about a month, according to the Julian calendar, pfft) before, but I figured I should give it a shot.

I turned on the TV, got in the shower, and stood under the warm water. I still felt nothing inside of me but my irregular heartbeat. I was just going through the motions, and April couldn't come soon enough. I turned off the water, got out of the shower—and that's when I heard the opening guitar riff. It was instantly infectious like nothing I had ever heard before. I could feel serotonin flooding my brain immediately. I didn't even put a towel on. I ran, still bare and glistening, into the room to see where these angelic sounds were coming from. Time slowed down. Had Mozart been reincarnated? Every second produced sounds better than the ones that came before. The ten-foot walk that felt like an arduous journey was complete, and I could now finally know whom to thank for this gift. I saw

Miley Cyrus, leaning on a car, singing the opening words to "Party in the USA."

"Shut the fuck up," I said.

I started dancing. Right when I needed a life raft from the universe, I got one. When it dawned on me that it was a teen Disney star who was giving me my life back, I started to laugh. It was the first time I had really laughed in months. That made me laugh harder. Then I started to picture what my mom would think if she happened to walk in the room to see me, wet and naked, laughing maniacally at a song for tweens, and that made me almost fall to the ground laughing. The laughter gave way to a stream of tears.

I'm aware that being alone in a basement, stark naked, soaking wet, and laughing hysterically with tears running down my face while "Party in the USA" plays in the background is also the makings of a "that's when I realized my destiny as a serial murderer" origin story. But this would be the first step in my road to recovery.

• • •

I'm proud to say that after that day I only did cocaine 113 more times in my life. Because the road to recovery is paved with relapses. That's what addiction is. You quit and you relapse. I often relapse because something bad happens. Well, something bad was about to happen.

After the Party in the USA I had in my mom's basement I wasn't suicidal anymore, but that didn't mean I was better. I still smoked weed all day every day, with a daily pack of smokes and four to eight coffees thrown into the mix. Not to mention binge drank until I passed out most nights. I had dropped 40 pounds when I was doing cocaine, putting me under 200 for the first time since high school, but I was creeping back up to that 200-pound marker again without my sanity-draining appetite suppressant. And I still lived in my mother's basement, without a dollar to my name, unable to hold back from spending all my money on substances instead of trying to move to Toronto. But the way I saw it was: if I'm not doing blow, I'm clean. I would leave parties if it was there, turn off movies that showed it, and even avoid bowls of sugar that resembled it.

"White-knuckling it" was a term originally meant to describe pilots clutching the controls of a plane so nervously and tightly their knuckles would turn white. Addicts use it to describe a kind of sobriety that is sustained by sheer willpower. You're not trying to fly the plane steady and straight, or fix any of the deep-rooted mechanical problems, you're just holding onto the controls and trying desperately not to crash. I was white-knuckling it for that entire first year off coke, but I did it. I got to November 1 and felt let down when it came. I had expected some kind of spiritual awakening on that day. Like I would know that shit was in my rear-view mirror forever. But it was just another day.

I did have an important career decision to make, though. When these kinds of things come up it's a total drag because half the reason I got into comedy was to avoid important career decisions. Howard from Yuk Yuk's wanted to sign me to an exclusivity contract. Yuk Yuk's had locations all over the country and could promote me nationally. Still, I felt loyalty to Absolute Comedy. That club gave me my start, and Jason had become a friend who forgave me for my meltdowns. I had to think of it like a business, and I needed advice, so I went to my guy.

"You're doing the right thing, ya hear me?"

"I hear ya. Thanks, Jocko."

"Anytime."

Without knowing it, Jocko was lying to me when he said "anytime."

Less than two months later, on the morning of my twenty-fourth birthday, while I was sitting on the toilet, I found out Jocko had died.

I woke up with a wretched hangover. I had learned a trick that would get friends to buy you "birthday drinks" for a full thirty-six hours if you timed it right. I speed-walked to the bathroom because my belly was full, as always, to the brim with booze and pizza. I figured reading all the birthday greetings on my Facebook wall would be a good way to start my day, but at the top of the news feed all I saw was comedian after comedian writing on Jocko's wall:

You'll be missed.

I can't believe you're really gone.

I thought he'd moved to the States or something. Until I saw three words that ripped my heart out:

Rest in Peace.

Jocko had died of a heart attack in his sleep.

That night, I relapsed on cocaine in a strip club.

● ● ●

When life gets tough, I choose the fog of getting fucked up, **every** time. After Jocko died I stayed in that fog for a couple months. I was doing cocaine in the same basement that I was in just over a year ago when I told Jocko that I would quit.

It was Jocko's death that pushed me into relapsing, but it was the memory of his life that pushed me into getting clean again. I would think of our talks in his car driving to shows when he would tell me I had to get my shit together:

The real hard work is done offstage when no one is looking.

Ali lived clean.

Nobody is going to fuck you if you're livin' in your mama's house when you're thirty.

The drugs don't work forever.

"I hear ya, Jocko."

For the second time in my life, I quit cocaine. It wasn't easy, but it was easier than the last time.

Just a few short months after Jocko died, I had to bury another loved one.

This time it was Bob. Look, I know this book has been a bit of a bloodbath so far, but if you really expected the dog to live forever, that's on you. I know he only appeared briefly at the beginning of the book and now I'm asking you to care that he died, but Bob was as big a part of my life as anyone you will read about here. The only reason he doesn't show up more is because we spent years secretly solving mysteries together and I'm still shopping around the rights to that story.

They say the great boxers age overnight. That's what happens to the great dogs, too. We lay together on the floor face-to-face, staring into each other's eyes, like we had done for countless hours when I was trying to quit cocaine. As he took his last breaths, I whispered through tears, "Thank you, Bob."

Later, my mom and I yelled at each other for the first time in years because she wanted a cigarette and I wouldn't give her one. She had finally quit smoking. She was a month in, and that was the longest she had ever gone, so, you see, I couldn't give her a smoke. I had never been more proud of her, and the last thing I wanted was for her to put this goddamn monkey back on her back.

"I'm gonna have a cigarette."

"No, you're doing so good."

"I'm just gonna have one."

"You know that's not true."

"Alex, give me a cigarette."

"No I'm not going to."

Then she yelled, "Give me a fucking cigarette!"

"No! You're going to do this over a fucking dog?" I yelled back.

It was a hurtful thing to say. I knew as well as anyone that referring to Bob as merely a dog was sacrilegious in our family. My mother was now sobbing and begging for a cigarette. Of course, I gave her one. And of course, she was a full-blown smoker again, immediately.

Now I'm going to have to do something else my editor warned me not to and skip ahead long periods of time in one pithy paragraph. But I don't know how else to cover from March 2011, when Bob died, to spring 2012, other than by saying this: I was fucked up for pretty much all of it. If I was awake, I was drunk or high. Usually both. I binge drank until I passed out six nights a week, always had a joint or a cigarette in my hand, started doing coke again, and even had a nice little opioid bender. Nothing specific triggered me this time. My motivation to stay clean had simply worn off.

What pulled me out of the throes of this relapse? I was sent overseas on a humanitarian mission to aid malnourished children by teaching them environmentally sustainable farming techniques. All right, fine, it was a local comedy competition. Do you know how much better I could make this book if not for this honesty thing? We could have been secretly prepping the first human colonies on Mars by now. Instead, I'll tell you about the Yuk Yuk's Ottawa Summer Comedy Competition.

Comedy contests are inherently unfair and not a true indicator of a comedian's talent. That's what I say when I lose them. But I won this one, so it was a utopian meritocracy that perfectly encapsulated the will of the comedy gods. When the first annual competition was announced I did something dumb that somehow led to something positive—a feat that is important for any addict to master.

I put way too much pressure on myself to win. I convinced myself that no matter who the judges were, where my spot in the show lineups were, or how many friends the other comedians brought: I needed to win the whole thing. I didn't want to make any excuses. I stopped drinking and smoking weed before my shows, and I stopped doing coke entirely.

Now here is where the dumb part of my plan comes in: I decided that if I didn't win this contest, I was going to give up trying to make comedy my career and become a full-time drug dealer. You can tell the stupidity of a plan by the stupidity of the backup plan. Suffice it to say, my backup plan was about as stupid as you can get without involving the word "hostages."

I placed first in the preliminary round and first in the semifinals. The night of the finals, there was a special guest judge: Mike MacDonald. Our paths had crossed a few more times since I was that kid he told not to be the last one to leave the bar. I found out that when Mike told me that, he was speaking from experience. He'd recently moved back to Ottawa because of health problems related to his younger days as a heroin addict and alcoholic. The drugs took twenty-plus years to catch up to him. Even though he'd been clean for a long time, there was a disease in his bloodstream that lay dormant for decades. He was diagnosed with hepatitis C and was on the wait-list for a lifesaving liver transplant. Mike started looking to me like the ghost of comedy future: thin, frail, and ghastly white. I could never tell if he remembered me, let alone liked me. Mike was hard to get a read on and often held court in the green room, mercilessly making fun of the comedian onstage.

Wafik was also in the finals. He went on a couple spots before me and slaughtered the room. I knew his would be a tough set to top. I managed to pull it off, though. I won, and Wafik was the runner-up. He told me after that he wasn't even upset because it's always a proud moment for a father when their son surpasses them.

Here comes a pathetic confession: winning that local pro-am comedy competition will always be one of the proudest nights of my life. Not because I won the contest, or the $500 that came with it. Not even because it meant I would continue pursuing my lifelong goal of becoming a professional comedian. I know it would be fitting for the purposes of this book to say it was because I did it without drugs or alcohol in my system, but that pesky honesty policy forces me to admit it wasn't that either. It was because of Mike's scorecard that night. He gave me 100/100. After we smoked weed in an alley together outside a comedy venue for the second time.

I moved to Toronto four months later, shortly after my twenty-sixth birthday.

PART 2

Alcohol

chapter 3

withdrawal

I'm about to die. My heart is beating chaotically and I'm sweating profusely. I've had these withdrawal symptoms before but never like this. I'm actually going to die.

The uncontrollable, bone-rattling shaking picks up again. Then everything goes black.

I don't know how long I was out, but when I come to I know I need help, and fast. I crawl, inch by inch, until I arrive.

"I need to go to the hospital," I say through my mom's bedroom door at three a.m.

My mother is up and at the door in less than twenty seconds. That's how she has always slept, ready to pop out of bed at a slight cough or knife-wielding kidnapper at a moment's notice.

• • •

"I turn twenty-nine tomorrow," I say to the emergency room nurse.

"Whoa! Did you just flash-forward three years?" she asks.

"Well, yeah. Wait, how did you know?"

"Because you were just talking about being twenty-six on the last page, and now you're twenty-nine."

"Twenty-nine tomorrow," I correct the fictional story-driving device I've just created.

"That would make today December 20, 2015."

"I'm glad I got a nurse who makes things so clear."

"Okay, well, let me just ask you some questions," says the sexy nurse, with pouty red lips and fishnet stockings under her uniform. She is clearly quite aroused by my presence.

"Is this really the most creative thing you could come up with?" the nurse asks.

"Hey, this is my fantasy here."

"I know, I'm just saying, women can be doctors too, ya know? I could be anything you want me to be right now and you're going to just go for the cliché sexy nurse trope? I could be someone from your past, the ghost of Abraham Lincoln, Buddha, or even some kind of alien being humans can't even conceptualize. Anything you could possibly imagine. Or you can go with the sexy nurse, you hack."

I stare blankly.

"Oh, for fuck's sake. Fine. But the second I hear the words 'sponge bath' I'm outta here. Where do you live?"

"Toronto. I'm just back here in Ottawa for Christmas. I finally moved out of my mom's house a few years ago and made the move to the big city to go after my dreams."

"Occupation?"

"Comedian. I'm headlining all over now. It's really exciting. I even got my first standing ovation this year. I'm sure Just for Laughs will have me back soon. I've never felt this confident about my career. I'm a real professional comedian. I also work at a call centre."

"Why are you in the emergency room?"

"I had a seizure, or something happened."

"And what happened in the three years before this?"

"I drank heavily pretty much every day, and I relapsed on cocaine earlier this year at a strip club in Montreal."

The nurse lowers her glasses and cocks her head to the side while holding intense eye contact with a look of complete indignation. "Any other medical conditions?" she asks.

"This year I had pancreatitis and a pilonidal abscess."

"A pilonidal abscess is a condition where a pocket of pus builds on the tailbone and must be drained with an incision under local anaesthesia administered with a spinal needle. They are known to recur and can be extremely painful."

"Maybe in layperson's terms for the reader?"

"You have a giant pimple on your ass."

"Okay, maybe not that layperson."

"Whatever you say, ass pimple. Want me to tell them what pancreatitis is?"

"Go for it. Just please don't call me ass pimple anymore."

"You got it, ass pimple. Pancreatitis is an inflammation of the pancreas that results in abdomen pain that varies from moderate to severe and can radiate around to the back. It is caused most frequently by alcohol abuse, but other risk factors are smoking and poor diet. Symptoms include pain, discomfort, rapid pulse rate, nausea, sweating, and digestive problems. Acute bouts of pancreatitis can be treated, but if the problem recurs, it can lead to chronic pancreatitis, which is a life-threatening condition that, best-case scenario, debilitates you for the rest of your days. Any sensible person who contracts an acute bout of pancreatitis learns their lesson and cleans up their life. All right, any other medical conditions this year?"

"Pancreatitis again later in the year."

"You don't need a sexy nurse right now. I think you need some tough love."

In an instant, the nurse transforms in front of me. His gold chains and earrings reflect the light, nearly blinding me. But I can still make out the unmistakable silhouette of Mr. T.

"Fool, how you gonna get pancreatitis twice in the same year?"

"I didn't plan on it. I really did try to quit drinking after the first bout."

"Then why didn't you, chump?"

"Well, I already had this other thing called a pilonidal abscess. Do you know what that is?"

"Yeah, I know what an ass pimple is."

"Well, the pilonidal abscess contracted a staph infection."

"Where did you get the staph infection?"

"A boxing gym."

"What does this got to do with drinking?"

"After the doctor told me I had pancreatitis from alcohol abuse I decided I would live a healthier lifestyle. I stopped drinking for an entire month while I was on the antibiotics for my pancreas. It was by far the longest I'd ever gone without drinking. I started training at a real boxing gym, just like I'd always wanted to. That's when the pilonidal abscess morphed into a staph infection."

"I feel sorry for the fool."

"Isn't the line 'I pity the—'"

"That's copyright infringement, boy. You take my intellectual property and I'll drop you."

"You know, I really think a nurturing-type character would be best for this part, so I'm going to have to bump you out, Mr. T."

"My word, that sounds terrible. What happened after all that?" says a loving Aunt May type.

"I started drinking heavily again."

"Why?"

"Because I had been doing hard drugs and drinking for fourteen years and I never got stabbed in the ass with a spinal needle in the ER from it. It was too hard. Thirty days of eating healthy and exercise and my body tried to kill me. I gave up and went on a six-month bender where I drank every night and had a dalliance with oxies, shrooms for dinner all summer, and a few MDMA trips."

"Those are some pretty hard drugs."

"The way I figured it, if I wasn't doing coke, I was clean."

"What happened leading up to the seizure tonight?"

"My pancreas had been hurting a lot again. Even more than before. I got drunk two nights ago and my pancreas hurt so much I couldn't even sleep. I thought it was going to burst in the middle of the night, so I decided to take a couple days off the booze. About an hour ago I just fell down shaking and blacked out. I woke my mom up and she drove me here."

Aunt May looks down at the floor. She looks back up and deep into my eyes. "Even heroes fall, my boy."

She places a brown paper bag on the foot of my hospital bed. I don't even have to look to know what's inside. I pull the mask over my face and web-sling out the window overlooking the city I've sworn to protect. Kingpin is out there somewhere, and I don't care if it takes all goddamn night—

I'm going stop right here because I know myself and this will just end up in Spider-Man erotic fan fiction for the next 100 pages. The real hospital visit that night didn't end with me being handed a superhero costume. Instead, I was given benzos for the withdrawal.

• • •

The first drink of alcohol I ever had ended up in the sink. I spit it out as soon as it hit my tongue. I tried to drink the whiskey straight, like a movie detective who just came home after finding a particularly gruesome murder. Being only fourteen, I needed to mix it with some pop, and that did the trick. I drank until I got drunk, and I got drunk until the room spun and I passed out.

The first twenty times I drank played out a lot like that first time. I drank until I passed out in bathrooms, arms around the toilet bowl in the universal sign for "her loss." I was drinking entire bottles of Jack Daniel's before I'd even kissed a girl, like a Benjamin Button of indecency. I loved everything about getting drunk. How it made my body numb and my thoughts dumb. The transformative power it had to change me from self-conscious to self-righteous. From alienated despair into too inebriated to care. Even if there were two of them, I actually liked the person staring back at me in the mirror when I drank. Alcohol made me not hate myself anymore—until the end of the night, when I was alone. But by then I was ready to pass out anyway, so what did it matter? To the detriment of the people around me, it also made me think I could sing.

I was better at drinking than I was at almost everything else. I dropped out of Carleton University and was kicked out of Algonquin College within seven months. I didn't finish school, but I did finish strangers' drinks at comedy clubs. As soon as the last audience member left the room I would race from table to table, slurping down all the unfinished drinks I could before the servers came to collect the glasses. It was the only time I was an optimist because I would see those drinks as half-full. Also because I would see them as not being tainted with mono. I was so gross I almost called this book *Martinis and Miracles: How I Avoided the Mumps.*

Casual drinking was never a thing for me. It was closer to casualty drinking. I'm a Canadian comedian who was raised Catholic—I never stood a chance. I didn't think of alcohol as a substance I used; it was one of life's necessities. Cigarettes, weed, food—I knew I abused all of those, too. But with booze it was never like that. How can you abuse something if it's part of the very fabric of your being?

You've heard about a lot of different physical withdrawal symptoms so far. Those symptoms are like a giant monster attacking a city. Just when you think this moth so big it blocks out the sun is the most destructive thing ever created, you hear the roar in the distance. It's miles away, but it still almost shatters your eardrum. Then you see the radioactive mutated dinosaur that is bigger than a high-rise, and a blue flame is shooting out of its mouth that turns entire city blocks into rubble. Alcohol withdrawal is the Godzilla of withdrawal. It features all the classics: shakes, sweats, dramatic body temperature swings, nausea, trouble eating, trouble sleeping, and headaches. But there's more—it causes seizures, like the one I had, and delirium tremens. Delirium tremens is considered the most severe of alcohol withdrawal symptoms. It's a full-body tremor that ignites a panic in your brain. Plain and simple, when the DTs kick in, you feel like you're going to die.

That's what the benzos are for. I spent my first seventy-two hours off alcohol in bed, drifting in and out of the DTs.

• • •

I had promised myself I would never been in withdrawal in this basement again. How did I end up back here? Is this who I am?

I had to call someone. It was the person who showed me that change isn't just something you get when you return your empties. You might be surprised to find out—it was my father.

A couple years after we almost fought each other in that moving truck in the thunderstorm, my dad showed me what we are all capable of.

"I'm just leaving the house," I said. "Do you want to talk to Kate?" It had become routine for me to avoid talking to my dad when he called.

"Actually, son, I wanted to talk to you, if you have a minute."

Really, old man? You're gonna fucking go through the motions for the millionth time and tell me that you've changed? That you're not that angry anymore? Save it. I'm not falling for this again. I'm not letting you raise my hopes that I might actually have a father who doesn't terrify me. Who doesn't beat me down into the ground and won't let me get back up. I'm not letting you do this to me again.

But that's not what I said. What said was: "Yeah, I have a minute."

"I know we haven't spoken much lately. And I know it's my fault." Usually, the first line of this speech was about how it was both of our faults. This new tactic intrigued me.

"Okay." I still wasn't ready to be fooled. I knew I had to circle away from his right hand because it always came. He draws me in with this shit, and then—*bam!* I'm knocked down.

"I'm sorry for what happened that day when you came to help me move. I'm sorry for so much more than that, too. I'm sorry for how many times I've said this to you. I know it might be hard to believe, but I've taken a long hard look at myself and I've changed. I'm trying to change, I should say. I'm sorry I ever made you feel like you had anything to do with this. It's always been my fault and only my fault. I understand if you're not ready, but I'm ready to be your dad again. I love you, son."

Fine. I'd go to his goddamn funeral. At first, that's all I felt this conversation had earned him. High praise for admitting it's your fault for the first time ever, Jim, but I'm not getting sucked into your shit anymore.

Over the next few months, though, I started talking to him again. Small stuff at first, hockey and boxing, mostly. Eventually, I agreed to see him again.

Many years ago, my grandfather and his friends built this cabin in the middle of the vast Northern Ontario woods. It's not even accessible by car. There's just a train track running through the bush, and you get off at your cabin without another one around for dozens of miles in either direction. Encounters with bears are a daily occurrence, and sometimes you might have to let them have your catch for the day, lest you became their catch for the day. I had been there once when I was eighteen, and I loved everything about it, except my dad being there. So when he asked me if I wanted to come up that spring, I skeptically said yes. I figured this was truly his last chance to show me that angry guy was gone. He had been great over the phone for months, but he had been great over the phone for years before that.

I arrived at the Greyhound station and my dad gave me a big warm hug. He was always a good hugger.

"Okay, we have to get to that train," he urged.

I took out a pack of smokes. "I just wanna have a cigarette before we go."

He didn't know I had become a smoker. I was fully prepared for a blow-up, and then I would get right back on the bus and go home.

"You can smoke in the car if you want," he said.

We talked non-stop the entire three-hour drive to the train and the two-hour train ride into the bush. We laughed and drank like two old friends who hadn't seen each other in years. Because that's what we were.

When we arrived it was about two hours before the pitch-black night would bring the curtain down on everything that wasn't six inches in front of us.

"Let's get on the boat for an hour before dark," my dad suggested.

We were already drunk, so we thought it was a great idea.

My dad got in the boat beside the motor, and I pushed us off into the water. It's tricky: you have to push out and jump in without capsizing the boat, and then the motor man has to start it up when you've made it into deep enough waters. I pushed off and jumped in, but as the boat started to make it to deeper water, we felt a sudden force stop us.

"Goddammit, you left the anchor on shore," my dad huffed.

Here we go. I jumped out of the boat, waded to shore, retrieved the anchor, and jumped back in, getting mud and water everywhere. We almost tipped and the motor got dangerously close to the rocks. But, as always, those concerns were secondary to my fear of the wrath that was about to befall me. My dad got quiet, and I knew he was seething. I braced myself.

He started to laugh. "I've done that before. Who would have thought going fishing in the dark while drunk wouldn't be a good idea?"

I don't know if he knew what happened in that old boat in the middle of the Ontario wilderness, but Jim became my dad again that night. In the years that followed there were times he lost his patience with me, but they were minuscule in comparison to his old ways and infrequent. I never thought people could change, but watching a forty-five-year-old man do it is the kind of thing that will make you a believer. Before, when I made mistakes, I tried to hide them from him to avoid his judgment and anger, but after that trip, I came to him with my slip-ups, confessions, failures, and relapses for understanding and wisdom. This man who used to yell at me from his hands and knees to show me the dirt I had missed sweeping is one of the first people I told about my cocaine problem. Don't tell me people can't change.

Now, freshly out of the ER, in alcohol withdrawal, feeling decidedly unrefreshed, I called my dad, and he was the first person I said it to:

"I think I might be an alcoholic." I still wasn't convinced ... But I wasn't unconvinced, either.

"I'll support you in any way I can," he said. "I get into Ottawa tomorrow. I won't drink for all of Christmas either. We got this."

I told him I was terrified this would destroy my career; sober comedian was almost an oxymoron in my view. Then he said something he would say to me a few times over the years:

"Person first, comedian second."

That was the only thing he didn't get. For me, there was no distinction between the two.

Here again, in this basement where I'd once made a suicide pact with myself, six years later, on my third day off alcohol, I made another pact with myself: I'm done with this shit. Finished. Finished killing myself. Finished wondering where nights, weeks, and years had gone. Finished regretting. Finished wondering what I could have been and not what I could still be. Finished hiding behind getting fucked up as an excuse for why I'm so fucked up, why I'm not where I want to be or who I want to be.

I felt like I was quitting the mob, walking into a dimly lit restaurant, sitting across from Vito Corleone, and telling him straight to his face, "I'm out."

• • •

It was my fourth day off of alcohol and five years to the day when, in this same basement, I had found out Jocko had died. That meant it was also another milestone.

"Happy birthday," my mom said, stretching out the words to be eighteen syllables.

On my eighteenth birthday I got kicked out of a club for being too drunk, and then passed out without a jacket in minus-thirty-degree weather on the hood of a car and nearly froze to death. On my nineteenth birthday I snorted two crushed-up pills of ecstasy and swallowed two more, and then rubbed my hands along my jeans for, a conservative estimate, five and a half straight hours. What I remember most from my twenty-fifth birthday was how many concerned onlookers asked me if I was okay.

This birthday was going to have more of a ginger-ale vibe, but I still wanted to have fun. I didn't even know if it was possible to have fun without hard drugs or alcohol, but I was going to find out. After dinner with my mom singing "Happy Birthday" with the enthusiasm of a child, I was off to my first sober birthday party since I was fourteen. I met my friends at our favourite watering hole and more than a dozen times that night had the following conversation:

"You're fucking kidding me, right?"

"Nope."

"Why?"

"Doctor told me I have to stop. I have pancreatitis."

"You mean like you're not drinking shots?"

"No, I'm not drinking at all."

"Okay, just a beer, then?"

"At all."

"Wait, just explain it to me one more time."

I could feel the shakes underneath my skin, so I headed to the bathroom for a benzo. No one pressured me to drink; my friends were just baffled. The evening was missing something, though. Something that could unite everyone in both revelry and revelation. A unique experience that brings everyone together as one.

"Strip club?" I suggested, without considering that two of my previous cocaine relapses had happened in strip clubs. This was a week of firsts and I wanted another one: first sober trip to a strip club.

When I ordered a ginger ale from the bartender at the strip club he rolled his eyes so hard I could hear it. I knew why. I'd seen people who drink ginger ales in strip clubs and they usually have their soft drink in one hand and the homemade Valentine's Day card for the dancer they're in love with in the other. I shouldn't make fun of them, I guess—they were, after all, now my people.

It wasn't five minutes after I took my seat in the front row before my friends decided I could use some company. I picked the dancer with the most sensitive-looking eyes and we headed to the couldn't-be-more-ironically-titled Champagne Room. It was day four off alcohol and I hadn't even been able to feel my penis the entire time. I had no sexual desire and was terrified that my genitals would lie dormant for the rest of my life.

I sat down in the booth that you always try to pretend you're the first person to sit in.

"You seem nervous," the dancer said.

"Sorry, I've never gotten a lap dance without being drunk," I confessed.

"I think you'll still have fun," she said.

Fears of a permanently broken penis were quickly resolved. My thought process went something like this:

Thank Satan, my dick still works.

Wow, that actually feels really nice.

Uh-oh.

No, please.

Don't you dare.

Oops.

Wearing khakis was a mistake.

I apologized to the dancer, and she replied that it "happens all the time." I quickly lifted my hands off the seat of the booth.

"Woody came in his fucking pants," Rob yelled to our friends, and the rest of the strip club.

The stain on my khakis was so noticeable it was like I was riding in JFK's car in Dallas.

On the embarrassment scale out of ten, ejaculating in your pants at a strip club is an eight. Ejaculating in your pants at a strip club while wearing khakis is a nine. Ejaculating in your pants at a strip club while wearing khakis and then having to refuse drinks that were bought for you because you aren't drinking is a hard ten. Having your friends buy you another dance to see if it will happen again and having it, sure enough, happen again? At least a ten and a half.

It was close to three a.m. when we decided to hit a late-night diner. We were the asshole table that was too drunk to be in a diner. If I'm being honest, we were kind of the asshole table that was too drunk to be in most places. We got a warning before we got our menus. I was laughing like a madman as a water fight broke out at the table. Full cups of water were being thrown with complete abandon, along with sugar packets and cutlery.

Water was splashing all over the place before I stood up to say, "Look, you got water all over my pants!"

On the cab ride home I was in complete amazement and bewilderment. I was a scientist who had just had their eureka moment.

It is possible to have fun without alcohol.

• • •

But on the heels of a tempting day came another one. My family does Christmas Eve a little different than most. 'Twas the night before Christmas, when all through the house, not a creature was sober, not even a mouse. The shots were poured carelessly into cups and a thick fog of weed smoke soon filled the air.

By the end of the night, I was dancing shirtless in the kitchen, but somehow, Christmas was the only spirit inside me.

I wasn't the only one celebrating a first that holiday season. It was my uncle Noel's first Christmas, which is also his birthday, in remission. Noel married into the hellscape that is my family by way of my aunt Kim, who was as loving and supportive as my mother, her sister. Kim and Noel had two children, my older cousin, Chris, and my younger cousin, Jessica. Our families were close, both emotionally and geographically, because they lived two blocks away from us. There were weekly dinners together, followed by board games accompanied by screaming and laughing. We were more like immediate family than extended. I looked up to Chris, and I was a far better older brother to Jess than I was to my own sister, Kate, when I was young.

The only person in their family I didn't feel close to—at first, anyway—was my uncle. Noel wasn't my blood. If you needed proof, he was quiet, even-keeled, and slow to anger. When we moved to Ottawa, he took me to my first professional hockey game, drove me to my hockey practices, brought me to my first wrestling show, and made me the best dinners of my childhood. Yet I only ever resented him as a kid. He would tell me to "Stop hitting your sister," "Help your mother more," and apply myself in school. I couldn't stand it. *You're not my fucking father*, I would think to myself. I would take all of his fatherly love and accept none of his guidance. But as I grew older we grew closer, and I started to see that he was only ever trying to help me. When I started stand-up he told me how proud he was of me for following my dreams, and he used to shake my hand with a fifty-dollar bill in his and tell me it was until I started making money in comedy.

Uncle Noel was diagnosed with stomach cancer just over a year before my first boozeless Christmas. It didn't even seem like that big of a deal. He was so calm, we just knew he'd be fine. He didn't even lose that much hair or weight. If cancer was a boxing match, my uncle dropped it like a bag of potatoes that he then lovingly prepared as a delicious side dish. My sister and I got Noel's family T-shirts that said *Team Noel. Fuck Cancer* in his beloved Steelers colours that year for Christmas.

This year we didn't even have to factor cancer into our presents. It was a joyous holiday, with the remission news and a new family member, Chris and his wife Jen's second daughter, Annabelle, so I didn't want to do what I had a history of doing: fucking it up. I made my brother, sister, father, and mother promise not to tell the rest of the family what was going on with me. I just wanted to have a normal Christmas and be with Vienna, Chris and Jen's other daughter, who was three.

"Alex," Vienna sang my name when we walked in the door.

Vienna and I immediately went to the basement to play, as we always did. There's a magic closet in my aunt and uncle's basement that transforms you into whatever you want. I spent an hour running away from a two-foot dinosaur with a runny nose. We played all her favourite games before us children were called upstairs for dinner. At the bottom of the stairs Vienna said we should race to the top. As I watched her run up the stairs, I was struck with an intense vision. It was of Chris and Jen having to sit Vienna down to tell her where Uncle Alex went. How I loved her very much, but she wouldn't be able to see me anymore. How they would try to explain an overdose or a ruptured pancreas to a three-year-old.

I was only thirteen days off the drink when New Year's Eve rolled around, but I wasn't stressing a dry end to 2015. New Year's Eve is different for comedians. It's a work night, one of the biggest of the year. But another difference is that we drink at work. If I'd made it through my birthday and Christmas Eve without drinking, this should be manageable. It was easy to not drink before the show because I'd already stopped doing that years ago when Mike MacDonald thought I could deliver a 100/100 set sober. His recognition convinced me to stop drinking before shows but certainly not after. No matter how a show goes, you want to drink. If you bomb and start questioning whether it's too late to go back to school, alcohol can be a great numbing agent.

But those times aren't even half as hard to resist as when there is real magic onstage. You are eliciting these titanic responses from hundreds of complete strangers using only your words. People are coming up to you and telling you how great you are. You forget about all the times you've failed, what the future holds, how much money is in the bank, and you're simply happy. I've come down off a lot of different substances, and nothing is harder to recover from than when you've lit up a crowd.

The New Year's Eve show was like that. I lit up the crowd, and afterwards, I was miserable. It was the first night that felt incomplete without drinking.

As miserable as I was, though, I knew I was making the right decision when I received my payment for the evening. I looked down at my cheque, and my brain did what it always did.

How much of this can we spend on alcohol?

It stunned me to know this was how my brain was wired, to think about money as only a middleman for substances.

That moment solidified for me that I had to quit drinking for good and for my own good. There was no turning back. Sobriety had given me the dexterity to finally open Pandora's box. I knew I couldn't lie to myself anymore and say that I just partied too hard. I'd said, "I think I might be an alcoholic" to my dad, but now I knew. That was my moment of clarity. I'm an addict. Somewhere along the way my life became solely about getting fucked up. I'd been a stand-up comedian for ten years and I still worked at a call centre during the day. I told everyone that comedy was my life, the most important thing in the world to me that I sacrificed everything for. It wasn't true. My addictions were the most important thing in the world to me and what I sacrificed everything for. Staring down at that cheque made it obvious: I'd given up my whole life for this shit.

chapter 4

playing the tape out

The next day I was on the subway back home in Toronto. I was carrying three heavy bags filled with Christmas gifts and every single possible item my mother thought I could squeeze in before I left. I think she got some dark matter in there somehow. I had made it through the shakes, a seizure, my birthday, Christmas, and New Year's without drinking. I even threw away my last benzo to prove to myself that I had changed. I heard my stop called and stood up, touching each pocket of my new coat to confirm I had everything. And then I felt the stress you can only feel when you touch an empty pocket where you weren't expecting to find one. I touched my breast pocket and felt nothing. I checked both side pockets and again met with emptiness. Panic set in. Where was my wallet?

I frantically began checking my bags. Nothing. I got off the subway and went to security to inform them of my missing wallet. They advised me to take the train all the way back across town to check if it was at the station where I got on. When I arrived there, the attendant at the booth had not seen my wallet. I got back on the train. Clenching my teeth and muttering obscenities to myself, I made a decision: I'm going to get drunk. Real drunk. I clearly can't deal with the intolerable burden of living without alcohol. I proved to myself I can cut back. I'm sure my pancreas will heal, just no more shots. I planned to go to the dive bar across the street from my subway stop. It was dark, no one talked to each other, the drinks were cheap, and there was a jukebox. It had been my secret hideaway from the world.

If I were a religious man, I would attribute what happened next to providence. I got to the front door of the bar, and a thought that had never entered my brain before in my life grabbed the microphone, cleared its throat, and loudly proclaimed:

Getting drunk won't help me find my wallet.

I had never even considered that alcohol didn't solve my problems. I dove deeper into this thought process.

If I get drunk, I'll just be a guy who's drunk with a lost wallet.

Those are the two most annoying things you can be simultaneously. I might as well just start listening to music on my phone in public without headphones and really complete the look. Plus, what happens after I get drunk? Am I going to score some coke because I'm so upset over a wallet? Will I feel better about my lost wallet when I'm hungover and strung out on coke tomorrow morning?

It was the first time I'd ever played the tape out. When you crave a substance your brain, if you let it, will get stuck in a loop that looks something like this:

I want this.

But I shouldn't have it.

I want this.

But I shouldn't have it.

You won't win that battle in the long run. Your knuckles can only get so white.

Playing the tape out means *thinking past* getting the substance you desire. Asking yourself questions: What happens *after* you consume it? How do you feel? Does your life get better? Why did you want this? How long did the pleasure from it last? Are you still happy you did it?

Playing the tape out would become my most important and most frequently used tool in battling addiction. The impulses in my brain that fire in nanoseconds did something I didn't know they could do. They slowed down when I played the tape out.

• • •

The next morning I woke up and went about my morning ritual. Staring at my phone while I lay in bed, bouncing between the same five websites that are harvesting my data and making the world a more divided place. It was how I always started my day; the only thing that varied was how much of this time was spent writhing in pain on the toilet atoning for the sins of the night before. I had a text from one of my agents, telling me that someone found my wallet on the subway and called him because his business card was in there. He gave me their number.

"Hello?"

"Hi, my name is Alex Wood. I was told you have my wallet?"

"Yeah, my girlfriend found it on the subway last night."

"That's incredible. Thank you so much!"

"I work downtown today 'til five if you want to come pick it up."

"Yeah, that would be great. Where do you work?"

After a pause he told me the name of one of the least reputable strip clubs in the city. I thought this whole not-drinking thing might work out after all.

Through the darkness and strobe lights I saw the DJ behind the booth, waving a wallet in the air. All the money was still inside, as well as my perennially maxed-out credit card. The DJ also refused any kind of payment—he just told me to pay it forward. Let that be a lesson: strip club DJs who work the day shift have hearts of gold.

My wallet felt like an Olympic medal in my hand. It doesn't make any sense, but I am convinced that the universe took my wallet as a test of my resolve—and I passed the test by abstaining from alcohol and was therefore rewarded with my wallet.

I walked confidently out of a strip club without booze in my system for the second time in less than two weeks. This time my pants were clean.

That first month off booze was nothing but strip clubs and hospitals.

I woke up groggy from the procedure and a nurse brought me into the doctor's office. I'd just had an endoscopy, which is an internal examination via a camera attached to a long thin tube. The doctor informed me that I had stomach ulcers. If you're keeping score at home, that's pancreatitis twice, a pilonidal abscess, a staph infection, and ulcers. All diagnosed within eight months.

The doctor told me I had to quit, in addition to alcohol, coffee, cigarettes, red meat, soda, candy, and dairy. I got home and chain-smoked.

When I was quitting cocaine and contemplating suicide, those items were high on my "reasons not to kill myself" list.

There was no way I could quit all of these at the same time. I started to walk to that dive bar hideout of mine. I got to the front door, just like I had two weeks earlier, and the same thoughts started running through my brain. I played the tape out, but it wasn't working this time.

Then I made myself a promise: *Just don't drink today. If you get through today, and tomorrow, and you still want to drink, you can drink.* It might not be the way they teach it in recovery programs, but that was the way I first learned what one day at a time meant.

The next morning I woke up and the decision I made is why you're reading this book. I didn't go to the bar. I went to a boxing class.

My dad had a heavy bag in his basement when I was thirteen. I would swing wildly at the bag for three-minute rounds with no regard for technique, and then sit back and be like, "All right, Everlast, come and get me." I mean Everlast the apparel and equipment maker, but I did also have a problem with Everlast the rapper at that time and was fully prepared to fight him. I was an Eminem fan and they were beefing, and the way I saw it was "If you got a problem with Slim Shady, you got a problem with me." I was really cool in grade nine.

Anyway, I figured the World Boxing Organization had to be getting wind of the legend of the self-taught kid in his father's basement that I had been crafting in my mind. I had no idea what I was doing, but I would hit that bag every chance I could with everything I could. It would be another fifteen years before I'd touch a heavy bag again, and that only lasted a month before the medical shit caught up to me. I'd always wanted to train, but there's not a lot of time for boxing when you're boozing.

This time, I was more committed to quitting booze, so I wanted to be more committed to boxing, too. There's only one place you should go if you want to be a serious boxer. A place where you go in a mortal but come out a battle-hardened warrior ready to take on all comers—the YMCA all-ages boxing class. All the YMCA greats were there: the old man who goes in the hot tub naked save for his socks, the couple trying to do more activities together because they have nothing left to talk about, the confused lady who arrives with her yoga mat and leaves when she figures out she read the schedule wrong, several small children, and the guy who is taking the class way too seriously (me).

Louis came in next and I knew right away this guy was the trainer. He was a five-ten bowling ball of muscle from French Canada with an infectious enthusiasm for self-improvement. Everything you want in a trainer. We started doing laps around the gym while he announced when to drop and do push-ups. It was my first time exercising in six months, and it showed. I'd have to look it up to be certain, but I'm pretty sure Sugar Ray Leonard didn't smoke a pack a day while training. There were looks of full-on concern from the rest of the class with every cough I let loose. I have to admit, if I were one of the other students, I'd also be concerned about the amount of sweat coming off the guy who, bewilderingly, brought his own boxing gloves. At the end of the laps, Louis came over and asked me if I was okay. I thought being the all-star in a beginner's YMCA boxing class was going to be embarrassing enough. I didn't consider what being the special project of the class would be like.

Suicide runs, push-ups, weighted punches, jumping jacks—and then the trainer yelled out the last thing you want to hear: "Okay, warm-up is over!"

I went into the hallway and vomited into a garbage can. Not to pat myself on the back, but if I'm not mistaken, that was the longest we've gone between pukings.

My next seven days revolved around boxing. I ran every day, and then I did push-ups, skipped rope, and beat on the heavy bag at the Y like my life depended on it. At night, I watched YouTube boxing technique tutorials and classic fights. I planned on being the YMCA all-ages beginner's boxing class champion of the world by Saturday. I was, at that moment, truly, the biggest fucking loser in North America.

Even before the end of warm-ups on Saturday I was sweating like the love child of Richard Nixon and Patrick Ewing. However, when I had the gloves and Louis was holding the mitts, he told me: "That left hook looks like you've been boxing your whole life!" Thank you, Fight Night for PlayStation 2.

After I recovered from the shock that apparently my best punch comes from my side with the lazy eye, I swelled up with pride. Class was still painful and unrelenting, but that comment got me by for the rest of it. On the walk home, I was probably feeling a little too good, as I had the following monologue in my head:

Okay, even though socks-in-the-hot-tub old man gave me a run for my money, I was the best in class today. I went from worst to first in one week. I'm twenty-nine now. After three years of intense training and rising up

the amateur ranks, I have my first pro fight by thirty-two, title shot by
my mid-thirties. It isn't inconceivable that I retire with an unblemished
record, having long ago watched the greats of the sport in my rear-view
mirror until they are barely visible dots and I'm left to compete against
only myself as the undisputed GOAT.

I don't think it's a spoiler to tell you the fight from page 13 is
not for the middleweight crown, but boxing helped get me where I
needed to go.

• • •

I was less than a year from my last coke relapse, less than two
months since I did hard drugs, and less than a month off booze, but
I decided I was going to write a book about addiction. An ambitious
idea for someone who was so freshly off those substances—and still
smoking weed and cigarettes all waking hours and washing them
down with pizza. It's like I was trying to write a book called *How to*
Become a Champion Swimmer, and the cover would be me wearing
PAW Patrol rubber arm floaties, a backwards Speedo, and a football
helmet. "Chapter 1: Did You Know You Can't Breathe Under Water?"

I sat down with a pen and pad and made a list of all my vices:
alcohol, weed, caffeine, nail biting, cigarettes, red meat, dairy, porn,
chips and candy, and social media. I was going to quit all of them and
write a book about it. That's what my 2016 was going to be—at least,
that was the plan. But like Mike Tyson once said, "Everybody has a
plan until they get punched in the mouth."

My new life was so clearly defined in my head, but there was only
one thing wrong. I was almost a month off alcohol, so I had no idea

why my hands still shook sometimes. More worrisome, why was the shaking spreading over my entire body? I thought they were DTs again at first, but these felt different.

I started seeing a neurologist, who ordered some tests and told me to remain patient because brain disorders can take a long time to be diagnosed. I'll tell you as much as I can about it as we go along, but I didn't know what was happening at the time, so, hey, why should you?

• • •

Monumental changes were happening in my life, but as always, the person took a back seat to the comedian. I had a dozen one-nighters in the next couple of weeks. A one-nighter is a one-night show that is not at a comedy club, usually not for a comedy-savvy audience, and a long drive away. It can eat your soul. You stay in motels that even fleabags would pass on, and some shows can really make you question if mime would have been the better career choice. Free alcohol at one-nighters is half the motivation I used to need to make the journey. I've always feared being alone and sober in a depressing hotel room on the road; it's a lot easier to just pass out. But the show must go on. Over the next two and a half weeks I spent upwards of forty hours in a car. As it turns out, being sober in a hotel room in a small town isn't that much different from being drunk in one. It was just another one of those things I used to romanticize. It's not like I was having Playboy Mansion–type parties in my room after shows, with dry martinis and a live pianist. I was passed out alone, covered in vending machine wrappers beside empty tall cans and handles of whiskey.

However, there was one show coming up that I was particularly dreading: the Thunder Bay Community Auditorium. I knew it would be my toughest test yet. In fact, I couldn't picture getting through it without drinking. It's hard to face an empty hotel room on the road sober as a judge (well, a judge who still smokes weed), and it's hard to come down off a stand-up show, bad or good, without booze, let alone for one of the biggest crowds I'd ever performed for (a 1,500-seat theatre). This was going to be a combination of all of those.

In terms of quitting drinking, I'm an up-and-coming contender who's only fought tomato cans. Tonight, in Thunder Bay, Joe Frazier is bouncing up and down and the sweat is pouring down his face, an intense thousand-yard stare in his eyes. Across the ring is me, wearing my glasses, with my mom wiping something off my face with a tissue.

"All right, Joe, this guy's got nothing," legendary trainer Eddie Futch says to his honed killer.

"Stop being fussy. You just have a few crummies I'm trying to get," my mom says as I squirm.

I'm going to go ahead and bring in the most famous boxing announcer of all time, Howard Cosell, for commentary: "Only four men have gone the distance with Joe. Frazier quite understandably the favourite."

I don't like my chances. I'm going into this show almost expecting to relapse.

At least I was working with my friends Daryl and Alex. Daryl has the best "I look like" jokes you've ever heard. He is sharp, ornery, and he does not suffer fools. I have no clue why he likes me. And sometimes I think Alex invented fun. The previous summer we did MDMA and stayed out until ten in the morning, hopping from illegal scary after-hours place to even scarier illegal after-hours place, laughing like drug-addled hyenas.

The three of us walked to the venue from the hotel, and I was feeling good. It was a beautiful space, with red velvet adorning the chairs and bright lights lining both balconies. A veteran stagehand who had worked at the theatre for thirty years told us about all the legendary comedians who had performed there: Bob Hope, Bob Newhart, George Carlin, Phyllis Diller, Rich Little, Norm Macdonald. Backstage, we were shown a giant fridge full of free booze, all for us.

Frazier comes out in his usual style, smokin'. His job is to get inside, his best weapon the left hook.

But when you have a burning pancreas and a stomach shredded by ulcers, the tape sometimes plays out on its own. I also reminded myself: I'm here to do comedy, not get drunk.

The greatest thing about theatre shows is how long you have to wait for the laughter to die down. In a club a big laugh can feel like a wave you're riding, but in a theatre it's a tsunami. You deliver a punchline and sometimes you have to wait a full fifteen seconds for the laughter to quiet so everyone can hear you say your next word. It feels like having a threesome with Euphoria and Contentment. This theatre show was no different. The other Alex and I kept telling the audience that the after-party was at Boston Pizza. It was a desperate ploy used by desperate comedians to try to get laid. After the performance, we got to Boston Pizza, and sure enough, there were three lovely women from the show. We broke the sound barrier with how fast we struck out with them. Daryl retired for the evening, but Alex wanted to go dancing.

I was afraid. Not because Thunder Bay is like the town in *Footloose* that outlawed dancing, but because Alex and I had danced in clubs, after-hours places, comedy bars, and anywhere else that is supportive of two men who dance poorly but passionately, and I didn't know if I could still do that without alcohol. I'd known for years that I could do comedy without it. After the holidays, I'd known I could have fun without it. But dancing without booze? That's against the laws of physics, isn't it? I studied physics in my spare time, not unlike Will Hunting, and was awarded an honorary PhD by Queen's University. Right, honesty. Fine, I googled this just now, but Archimedes' principle states, "When a body is partially or totally immersed in a fluid, it experiences an upward thrust equal to the weight of the fluid displaced." I'm not completely sure, but that certainly reads to me like "You have to be real hammered to dance." So I decided to find out what would happen when my unstoppable force of quitting drinking met the immovable object of trying to boogie.

We ended up at a place with a live band and a massive dance floor, but everyone was just sitting at tables and watching. Like two kids staring at perfectly still water, we couldn't resist the urge to cannonball. With every eye in the place on us, we walked to the dance floor, straightened our collars, and let loose. Now, in our minds, the whole place was just waiting for someone to do it so they could join in, and we figured the dance floor would quickly fill up after we broke the dam, and then we'd be carried out on their shoulders. But after three songs of just the two of us giving it our all, that didn't seem to be the case. Alex and I danced like contestants in a dystopian game show who would be put to death if they stopped. The floor *finally* filled up with a mass of bodies, and I turned down dozens of drinks from people who were at the show earlier.

He's getting into Frazier's head. I think he hurt Joe Frazier. I think he is hurt.

We danced for so long I can't be sure that I'm not still there and everything that has happened since isn't a dance-induced fever dream. Last call came and went. The lights that remind you there is an entire world you forgot about outside of these walls turned on. The band thanked us for getting the place hopping. People were slapping us on the back and thanking us for the show earlier and the dancing just now. We could have run as co-mayors of Thunder Bay and won in a landslide.

We walked back to the hotel, gushing about what a great night it was, beginning to end, as hundreds of thousands of perfect snowflakes fell under a blanket of bright stars. Then the best part happened. Alex complained about how hungover we'd be tomorrow, before he stared at me in complete shock and said, "Oh, that's right. You didn't even drink tonight."

Down goes Frazier! Down goes Frazier! Down goes Frazier!

chapter 5

two fighters

I filled the glass right to the top until it almost overflowed, the way I always did. The next step was chugging it back, but on this particular February morning I paused to marvel at it first. How could I have spent the last month, let alone my entire life, taking this for granted? Billions of people are literally dying for water, and I can have it anytime I want. I've spent most of my life thinking I was cursed, but am I really? I thought of my worst moments of addiction—they had all happened to me while I was safely housed in my mom's basement. I don't think it can really be a curse if your personal hell is a McMansion in the suburbs of Ottawa. It's not an admirable trait to have to fess up to, but I can be a bit of an ungrateful, miserable prick. I tend to focus on what I don't have, instead of what I do. I fixate on what's going wrong, instead of what's going right. But it wasn't just this glass of water that taught me gratitude; it was my new roommate, Mo.

Moaiad, or Mo for short, was a charming young guy and the hardest worker at the best shawarma shop in Toronto, Laziza. I'd first gotten to know him when I would drunkenly order two shawarma wraps at a time. This honesty shit is tough. Make that three shawarma wraps at a time. He was always blaring Notorious B.I.G. and would make fun of me for how much food I ordered. I liked him right away. He came over to check out the place where I was living when I was interviewing potential roommates just before I quit alcohol.

When I told him I had a lot of applicants coming by, Mo looked me in the eyes and said, "You cancel on them and tell them you found your guy."

So I did.

The first morning he came downstairs to see me hitting a pipe filled with weed.

"Yo bro, do you smoke crack?" he asked.

"No, why?"

"Sorry, it's just—it's ten a.m. and you're smoking this pipe and you're always so fucked up when you come in the restaurant."

I'd told Mo about some of the unbearable hardships I'd faced in my life, and then he told me about his life.

"I know it can be tough. Bro, I grew up in a Palestinian refugee camp."

What? I hadn't known that.

"I have seen my family killed by soldiers in front of my face when I was just a small kid."

Oh man, I really wished he went first.

"But now, I'm here in Canada. I'm happy. I look outside and I don't see tanks in the street; I see smiling faces."

He was right when he told me that I'd found my guy.

As roommates, we chain-smoked, drank coffee, and laughed for hours. Growing up, our lives were similar yet starkly different.

We both remembered the troublemaking of our youth, but while my friends and I were throwing eggs at cars and running away, Mo and his friends were throwing rocks at tanks. This guy was working seventy-five hours a week to send money back home to his family. He was always awake before me, smoking a cigarette and staring out our living room window. It was from this spot that he would constantly drop pearls of wisdom, that I would internalize and use as a mantra. Two things he said will always stick out.

One day, he was filibustering about the past, and he just blurted out, "Today is the only thing."

The other one happened when I saw him in his usual spot one morning, but this time, as he was staring out the window, there was a different intensity in his gaze.

I said, "It's like you're looking for something."

"My friend, I am looking for someone, not something."

He took a deep haul from his cigarette. I knew some majestic answer was going to come out. He was going to say he was looking for God, wasn't he? Or better yet, himself.

He blew the smoke out of his mouth, and without breaking his stare out the window, he said, "Beyoncé."

Mo moved in with his cousin closer to the shop a few months later, but we stayed close. To this day, I still keep an eye out for Beyoncé for him.

• • •

Playing the tape out and learning mantras had been doing wonders for my battle with alcoholism, but now I had two more tools at my disposal: water and gratitude. There would be more to come.

"Why don't you try drinking tea? It really calms you down, and it's good for you," my mom said when I called her to grouse about quitting coffee.

I grabbed the first box in the store that said *caffeine free*, brought it home, and took my first sip of peppermint tea. I was soothed, relaxed, focused, and felt high on being not high. I sat back with my cup and thought about all the progress I had already made. The hot liquid warmed my insides, coursing through my body like a healing elixir for every stress and anxiety. I can't lie to you and say it felt as good as the first time I did cocaine. But it was better than the last time.

I can't tell you what single moment gave me awareness of my thoughts. The first time I ever did boxing mitt work, everything but me was too fast. The speed was blinding. My opponent was circling, and I was supposed to slip a jab, then slip a straight, and then follow that up immediately with a jab and a straight of my own. Pretty basic stuff, really. But I kept tripping over my own feet. I was dropping my gloves. I was bending my waist, not turning it. I was in range when I should have been out and out when I should have been in. I could slip the jab all right by the end, but the cross behind it always got me, even though I knew it was coming—and the punches I threw back were awful. There were just too many things going on at once and too much for me to do.

But the second time I did mitt work, everything moved a little slower. I got hit a little less, and I hit a little harder. It's not that anything was actually moving slower; I was processing it all in a way that made it feel like it was. You can guess where I'm going with this.

Something similar had been happening in my brain since I quit drinking. It was the complete opposite of what I had expected from a lack of alcohol. Anxiety, impulses, anger, and thoughts of hating myself were all more manageable. It felt like they were all moving slower and my logic was moving faster. And you know what they say in boxing—speed kills. I had always anticipated having a mental breakdown if I were to quit drinking. Two months in and I had never felt more sane.

March brought with it the arrival of one of my best friends back in Canada. Dylan and I look like we could be blood relatives, plus we like and dislike the same things, which makes it odd that we make fun of one another tirelessly and mercilessly whenever we're together. Dylan moved to England the previous year because Canadian crowds had finally thrown too many rotting vegetables at him in protest of his act. He was coming back for a month, and I'd agreed to see him because I felt bad that everyone else hated him. We had a gig co-headlining in Ottawa that I was excited about. I was also a little nervous. As much as I love Dylan, our relationship had always been predicated on getting drunk together.

The first time we met was at a comedy club on a rainy night years ago. The show ended and Dylan came up to me and said, "I have some whiskey. You wanna go drink it in an alley?"

"Yes, I do," I replied.

We went to the alley behind the club and finished his bottle of whiskey, chain-smoking under a small overhang. Our relationship carried on that way for years, and Dylan has always been my favourite person to get fucked up with. I was worried that maybe I'd be weird around Dylan. Or he'd be weird around me. Or we just wouldn't click the same way. Or, worst of all, that I'd just say, "Fuck it" and drink.

I met Dylan at the Greyhound station in downtown Toronto bound for our shows in Ottawa. He was with his girlfriend, Alexis, whom I adore. She's hilarious, empathetic, smart, and clearly punches down to date Dylan. The three of us always have fun together. We boarded the bus, where there was an agitated man who started pacing in the aisle shortly after we got on the highway. As he got close to me, he nudged my bag with his foot a little bit.

"Move that," he said.

I begrudgingly moved my bag a little farther under my seat. He told us he was on an all-protein diet and would be using the bathroom frequently.

Meanwhile, Dylan and Alexis were singing loudly and acting like toddlers on a road trip. It was quite entertaining, but I was aware that the rest of the bus hated us. Plus, our pacing friend was now seated a couple of rows ahead, staring back at us angrily and muttering. Dylan and Alexis started exchanging grade-seven-style yo mama jokes. After Dylan told one involving high heels being an oil derrick of some kind, the menacing man with too much protein in his system turned all the way around in his seat.

"That was a terrible joke. I've got a good joke for ya," he said with a slight grin.

He proceeded to tell us a joke that is unprintable even in a book with as many juvenile one-liners as this one.

Then he said, "I wanted to apologize for my behaviour earlier."

That surprised us.

"I just got out of prison."

That greatly surprised us.

"Inside, that's just how it is. I just got let out a couple of weeks ago."

The other passengers on the bus all shifted in their seats in unison.

"How long were you inside for?" Alexis asked.

"Ten years," he replied.

I could see people's faces growing more concerned as they thought about which non-violent crimes might come with a ten-year sentence.

"It was for assault. I should have known better," he said. There was now no way for the people on this bus to feel any less comfortable.

"Plus, I had priors."

Well, I stood corrected.

"Welcome back, man," Dylan said earnestly.

"It's good to be out. I know this is a long bus ride on the boring highway, but for me this is great. Just looking outside and seeing the sky, green grass, and the sun. I'm lucky."

I was doing it again before this bus ride—looking at this weekend with nothing but pessimism because I wouldn't be able to drink and thinking about what I wouldn't have. So I started thinking about what I did have. I was with one of my closest friends on the way to go live out my childhood dream, and I was getting paid for it. I took a big drink of water and felt like maybe there were two lucky guys on this bus.

• • •

Later that night, Dylan and I were walking down the street to the club.

"I need a peppermint tea before the show," I said.

"Peppermint?"

"Yeah, I've been experimenting with the fruit teas lately, but I need a solid peppermint right now."

"Dude, why not just start growing the ponytail right now?"

The next day I went to Dylan and Alexis's hotel room, where they surprised me with a present. A box of herbal teas from a fancy tea shop. I thanked Alexis, but she assured me it was all Dylan's doing.

Not everyone is going to support you when you quit drugs or alcohol. In fact, some may doubt, slander, or outright abandon you. I'm going to tell you something about those people. Fuck them. You don't need people like that in your life. Lots of people gave me a hard time when I told them I was quitting drinking. I noticed two things about *those* people: I never much cared for them to begin with, and they had based their entire persona on drinking or getting high. Even when I was a coked-up drunk, I thought those people were the dullest humanity had to offer. They're adults trying to be the coolest kid in grade ten. Drop those people.

The other kind of people who may not support you are raging addicts. I've experienced them to be mostly supportive; they may even ask you for advice on how you did it. But the ones who ridicule or shame you for your sobriety may as well be making a clicking noise with a spool of film running out of their ass because they're projecting. They wish they could do what you're doing, but they can't.

Every boxer who was undefeated for a long time but then suddenly had their air of invincibility taken away from them after a brutal loss says the same thing. They started to see who their real friends were. Who was there for the glamour, the money, and the party—and who was there for them. You'll be surprised to discover there are way more people than you expected in the latter group, I swear it.

I thought spending the weekend sober with one of my best drinking buddies would be a hurdle. Instead, it was a stepping stone. Discovering that Dylan, and so many others, wasn't one of *those* people made me feel less alone. Also, I'd like to boast this is probably the best instance in history of someone having an impassioned stance on "those people."

Despite that happy discovery, however, after I got back from the weekend with Dylan and Alexis, I dropped out of the pink cloud. The "pink cloud" is a term used in recovery circles to describe what a lot of people go through at the beginning of quitting drugs or alcohol. You feel invincibly confident, not just about sobriety but about everything. It essentially means being high on life. For more than two months I had felt like I was mainlining life into the tip of my penis. It can be great for getting you through the beginning stage, but then the pink cloud fades, and it starts to feel like work to stay clean. For the first time since I quit, it was becoming a slog to get through the day without booze.

The temptation to drink gnawed at me for weeks. It's a harsh hit of reality when every night without alcohol stops being a cause for celebration and you can't numb your brain to turn off the world when it isn't to your liking. It sucks because you thought the hardest part was over. In a way it is, but just because the hardest part is over doesn't mean it isn't hard.

So I decided to go to an Alcoholics Anonymous meeting. I was hoping against hope that it would be a one-time quick fix, and I prayed to God they wouldn't talk about praying to God. It was in the basement of a church, and I was late because I stopped for a peppermint tea on the way. I tried to sneak in, but it felt like the entire room saw me enter and could smell the freshness of my sobriety. The people were all welcoming. Too welcoming. I shook my head every time someone offered me the chair beside them. It's like they knew I wanted to run out of the place. I left not having made eye contact, let alone spoken, with anyone.

For a while, I went to about a meeting a week with my friend Marito. He's a comedian from El Salvador who was raised in Canada. He's five-two and jacked with muscles, and he can start a dance party anywhere—the world is his Thunder Bay, but in a good way. He's unwaveringly positive in an industry teeming with negativity. His likeability borders on mystical. Until he gets drunk. We bonded over hip hop, dancing, disciplinarian fathers, and alcoholism. He'd been sober six months longer than I had. He loved AA, but I just couldn't get behind it the same way he did. There was too much talk about God. When you have the relationship with God that I do, or did, you don't really have much to say to him anymore. Instead, peppermint teas with Marito came to be my personal AA. Those first few months he talked me through the tough nights, and we did boxing drills during the day.

We become *hermanos*, and that made it tough to watch what Marito would do to himself a few months down the line. But that's in the future. For now, like they told me at the meetings, one day at a time.

It was a good thing I had gained a new comedy brother because around that time I lost one, too. Wafik told me that quitting drinking was stupid. He told me that I wouldn't be able to do it. I knew to be on the lookout for *those* people, but I didn't think one of them would be the guy who called himself my comedy dad.

"I don't know how we're going to be friends anymore," he said to me.

I didn't tell him, but neither did I.

• • •

Towards the end of winter, I was headlining in Ottawa. I may have dropped out of the pink cloud, but cloud nine was there to break my fall. I came offstage after my forty-five-minute set, and when I got to the green room, there was Mike MacDonald. In the years that had passed, against the odds, Mike had overcome his illness and received a lifesaving liver transplant. He came close to dying, but he was back to killing. He wasn't on the show tonight, though, so I was confused to see him.

"Hey, Mike, what are you doing here?"

"I came to watch you."

A man who did Just for Laughs twenty-seven times and the *Tonight Show* with Johnny fucking Carson spent his Saturday night watching me. I was frozen. I didn't know what to say. I stood there staring in disbelief for a few moments.

Mike put his hand on my shoulder, smiled, and left.

• • •

There's an old saying in boxing: it's the hits you don't see coming that hurt the most. I wasn't much a fan of St. Patrick's Day to begin with. Don't get me wrong, I always loved a society-wide excuse to pass out in a bathtub covered in vomit, but I always hated how St. Paddy's Day crowded the bar with lightweights. I didn't need a saint to give me permission to get annihilated on a Tuesday morning.

That particular St. Patrick's Day, I grabbed my boxing gear and headed to the gym as usual. I put my hand wraps on, and before I slipped on my gloves, I got a call from my mom. She was barely able to get the words out her voice was shaking so intensely.

"Your uncle Noel's cancer is back. It's terminal."

I tried my best to console my mother, hung up the phone, and instantly began to wail on the heavy bag with just my hands wraps on. It wasn't long before I stopped, grabbed my stuff, stormed out of the gym, and started to walk to the bar. Then I remembered my last walk to the bar and my new emergency tool. I told myself not to drink today, that if I still wanted to in the morning, I could. But it didn't work. *I'm drinking. I don't care.* I was aware of my thoughts, they were moving slowly in a time of crisis like they never had. Those last words kept playing in my brain: *I don't care.*

What do you not care about when you say that? You don't care about your family and how they're doing with this news? You don't care about them getting a call saying you're in the hospital with a ruptured pancreas, and now two loved ones have poison filling up their insides? You don't care if you're the fuck-up who's always putting himself and his addictions first for the rest of his life? For fuck's sake, you just found out your uncle is dying and you've barely thought of him. You've only thought of yourself and your addictions.

Turns out, I did care. I turned around, went home, and drowned my sorrows in a cup of peppermint tea.

A week later, they cut my uncle open to see if a miracle could be performed. Instead, they came out with a death sentence. My uncle had weeks to live.

But Noel had other ideas. He told everyone that he was going to make it to see his granddaughter Annabelle's first birthday on July 1, months later than the doctors told him was possible.

If my uncle was going to fight, so was I.

chapter 6

wish you were here

After only three months off booze I was able to quit my day job at the call centre. I was making my way in the world solely off the money I earned from making people laugh. Quitting drinking had literally made my dreams come true. I can't tell you the satisfaction of telling people you're a comedian, and when they respond, "Yeah, but what do you do for work?" just repeating, "I'm a comedian." Don't get me wrong, the satisfaction goes right out the window when they immediately follow that up with "Tell me a joke."

During this period, I was in only one of three places: a comedy club, the gym, or with my family in Ottawa. I added twenty minutes of new material to my act about quitting drugs and alcohol. I was tighter and more consistent onstage than ever. When I found out, for the seventh year in a row, that I wouldn't be going back to Just for Laughs, it didn't lead to a meltdown bender like it had the previous six years. It made me dig in my heels and work even harder. I was at the gym six days a week, diving deeper into boxing, learning everything I could. It was the first thing besides comedy I'd ever worked hard at. Instead of trying to find a place to score drugs on the road, I was now trying to find the boxing gym.

Every few weeks I travelled home to see Noel and the rest of my family. As I was getting stronger, he was getting weaker. But we had one thing in common: we were both fighting towards a goal. We had never expressed deep emotions to each other, but if there was a time to do it, it was now. While I was on a train heading back to Toronto after a visit I sent my uncle the following text:

Hey, Uncle Noel. I wish I didn't wait until times were tough to say this. I just want to say thank you for everything you did for me and my family. I wasn't happy when my family split up and moved to Ottawa, but I remember being excited when you'd bring me on adventures in the back of that old station wagon. Taking me to hockey practices, my first NHL game, my first wrestling show, movies, and dinners. I didn't appreciate it at the time. I know we aren't blood, but you are like a second father to me. I love you.

Within minutes I received this reply:

Thank you, Alex. I've always thought the bond between our families was something special. We feel like immediate family more than extended family. I'm happy to see you doing what you love with your life. I'm proud of you and I love you too.

About a month before Annabelle's birthday, I got the news. Muhammad Ali was dead. For the first time in my life, the champ wasn't there. As we ran laps at boxing class that afternoon, Louis and I shouted, "Ali, *bomaye!*"—the spontaneous cheer "Ali, kill him!" Congolese audience members sang as the once-and-future champ prepared to fight a seemingly invincible George Foreman in Zaire. After class, I watched Ali do the impossible and beat Foreman in *The Rumble in the Jungle* for the millionth time. That day, I got my "Rumble, young man, rumble" tattoo on the back of my left shoulder. I figured there was at least one promise to my past self I should keep.

Over the coming weeks, I would need some of Ali's strength, or at least his ability to take punishment. It was Canada Day and I was in Ottawa. My new landlord informed me over the phone that I was being illegally evicted from my apartment in Toronto. It was overcast with rain clouds, and I had two pool parties that day. The first was an annual extravaganza that my friend Al had been hosting for ten years, ever since he won our first hockey pool; it's called the pool-pool party (some victory laps never end). My friends were shocked to discover that I was still not drinking. But sobriety and being an adult didn't stop me from honouring a yearly tradition.

I took the ladder from the garage and climbed to the roof of Al's parents' house. The twenty-five feet from the roof to the pool looked a lot higher without booze or drugs in my system. A bird nearly flew into me as I dropped down into the water. The party was fun for a while, but I ended up leaving early and irritated because I was continuously offered drinks. Al's bachelor party was coming up in a couple of weeks, and it was clear to me that I might have to skip it.

There was another party that day I was looking forward to more anyway: my cousin Annabelle's first birthday. My uncle reached his goal. It was a huge party with dozens of family members who had come to Ottawa from all over for "Annabelle's birthday party." It may have officially been called a birthday party, but we all knew it was a goodbye party.

My uncle may have been sick, but he wasn't too sick to chastise everyone when they were on the dry deck in a wet bathing suit.

"We need some music. Do you have any speakers?" I suggested when night fell.

"Great idea. There's two portable speakers inside," Uncle Noel replied.

There was almost no room on the pool deck for people to move, but the noisy buzz of conversation died down when I said, "All right, Uncle Noel. You're the DJ. What do you want to hear?"

Without hesitation he responded, "Pink Floyd, 'Wish You Were Here.'"

There's a difference between a silence and a hush, which is what washed over every single person in the backyard when Noel said those words. Then the haunting opening chords to one of my all-time favourite songs started to play. In a year of so many firsts, I was about to witness the most powerful one of all. My graceful, quiet uncle, whom I had never seen make so much as a toast at a holiday dinner, stood up.

His eyes were exhausted and filled with tears, and his voice trembled as he said, "I want to thank you all for coming tonight, and I want to thank you for making my life worth living. I love you all very much. Promise me you'll take care of my Kimmy after I'm gone. I don't want to be forgotten, and I hope that from now on, when you hear this song, you'll think of me."

Two weeks later, I relapsed at Al's bachelor party.

Two weeks after that, my uncle Noel died of cancer.

He took his last breaths in the same room where we'd opened presents for so many Christmases and birthdays. The same room I was pacing in as a terrified eighteen-year-old when my mom walked in and just knew that I was on my way to perform my first ever comedy set.

I was upstairs playing with Vienna when it happened. Later that day, everyone was eating dinner outside on the deck when she noticed her grandfather's sunglasses on the table.

"Oh no!" she said. "God forgot Grandpa's sunglasses when he took him to heaven."

It was the only time I can remember being happy at the mention of God.

During that time, I tried my best to be as strong as my cousin Chris. I had always seen so much of my uncle in him. When we all needed Noel the most, Chris was there: cooking, cleaning, consoling, with the same quiet grace. I was honoured when my aunt Kim asked me to be a pallbearer at Noel's funeral. I stayed in Ottawa for an extra week, babysitting Vienna for so many hours that the curtain was pulled back for me to see, truly, what a complete fucking nightmare full-time child care can be. Instead of putting my addictions first, I put my family first.

Then I went back to Toronto and put my addictions first.

PART 3

Alex Wood
Quits Everything

chapter 7

april fool

April 1, 2017, was the day I recorded the first episode of my podcast:

"You are listening to *Alex Wood Quits Everything*. I'm a recovering drug addict and alcoholic, and over the next 365 days I'm going to quit the rest of my vices. I quit something new on the first of each month, and they all continue over. The things I'm quitting are: weed, caffeine, chewing my nails, red meat, dairy, cigarettes, porn, social media, credit cards, gossip, smartphone, and sugar. Only one rule: no relapses. This is going to suck."

The months leading up to this recording were some of the toughest of my life. I was homeless, heartbroken, grieving, relapsing, and couch-crashing. I went to Al's bachelor party and took MDMA, ate dairy and red meat, and smoked weed and cigarettes (after white-knuckling it for five days without them). Somehow I made it through the night without drinking, but I was a pothead who chain-smoked again by the next morning.

I decided I would do MDMA every few months. Unless you have a strange habit of starting books right in the middle, you'll probably be able to guess that I didn't keep to that schedule.

I was still in the throes of my MDMA bender when I watched boxing trainer Virgil Hunter yelling at his pupil between rounds. Andre Ward is an Olympic gold medallist and surefire future Hall of Famer. But he was overmatched in this particular fight. Sergey Kovalev was the most feared puncher in the division. He was an undefeated Russian knockout machine, and he knocked Ward down early in the fight. The outcome looked to be academic at that point. But between rounds, Hunter said something to Ward: "This is what greatness is. Robinson got up. Leonard got up. Ali got up. You got up. Do it." Andre Ward had a comeback for the ages and won the fight to cement his place as an all-time great.

I did MDMA for the next forty-eight hours straight and continued my downward spiral. I told my family about my relapse so I would be accountable to someone because I knew I wasn't to myself. But there's only so many times your family can tell you they're proud of you for admitting you have a problem before you start to hear the pain outweigh the support in their voices. I had pushed them past that point.

I kept waiting for something special to come along, like that Miley song years ago. Or rousing words of perseverance from a wise and grizzled boxing trainer. I would even have settled for an inspirational meme from an Instagram influencer. Anything that would speak directly to my soul and motivate me to pick myself up and claw my way out of this shit one last time.

It never came. I knew this time it was on me. I had to learn the difference between motivation and discipline.

I had always been an undisciplined person who was easily motivated. It's relatively easy to get motivated; it's much harder to get and
stay disciplined. Discipline, though, can be learned. It can be learned
the same way you can learn to throw a good one, two. Repetition.
Throwing 100 bad jabs just to throw a good one. Despite everything
boxing had taught me, before this moment, there was always one
aspect of the sport that I'd never really taken into my brain: you're
going to lose. It's not about why you lost, or even how many times.
It's about how you come back from losing. That's where true greatness is. Relapsing always made me feel like I had lost. I started to
think about it in a different way.

Relapsing isn't going backwards; it's going sideways, which
isn't the same thing at all. Sideways means you're off the path, yes.
Sideways means you lost ground moving forward, yes. But it doesn't
mean you've gone backwards. It's a scientific fact that halting something's forward momentum doesn't immediately make it travel
backwards. Unless you, like, murdered a family in a drunken rage.
That should probably count as travelling backwards. But look, unless
you're the Strangleville Strangler, it's not too late for you. I realized it
wasn't too late for me. I was restarting, starting all over again. Again.

Still, this realization wasn't enough. I smoked weed like a madman and cigarettes like I was on *Mad Men*. I constantly ate the foods
and drank the coffee that caused me unrelenting pain and ripped
further holes in my stomach lining. My credit card was nearly maxed
out again. I chewed my nails more than I chewed vegetables, and I
could no longer attribute that fact to efficient smoothie-making. On
my phone, I'd flip between Tinder, Facebook, and porn for hours,

just hoping that one of these times it would rid me of the crippling loneliness I now felt all the time.

So I resolved to quit everything I was going to quit the previous year and more. Weed, caffeine, nail biting, cigarettes, red meat, dairy, porn, credit cards, gossip, sugar, social media, and my smartphone. It would be a full detox. Then I would see which things I wanted in my life, just in moderation. Maybe everything didn't have to be all or nothing.

Since I'm a comedian, and legally mandated to have one, I was going to do it as a podcast this time. I thought writing a book might be too hard for me to accomplish.

I was going to get and stay sober, which in turn would inspire other people to do the same. I was going to meet someone and fall, at warp speed, into an all-consuming love. I was going to get invited back to Just for Laughs, and this hurt inside me would be gone for good. No biggie. And if none of that happened, that was okay, too, because at least I was going to fucking try.

The next day I maxed out my credit card, like I had done so many times before. But this time it wasn't for drugs and booze; it was for a laptop and a microphone. The day after that, alone in my bedroom, I poured my heart out for that first podcast episode. It took me five hours to get through it without breaking down. But I had the discipline to try again after every failed attempt.

And I quit weed on April 1, 2017. Seven years to the day after I'd once planned to end my life.

chapter 8

weed

I can't sit here and tell you that weed is as harmful as cocaine and alcohol. I can't pretend I'm not all for the legalization of weed for its proven medical benefits. I also can't sit here and say that weed hasn't had negative impacts on my life or pretend that I haven't spent what would amount to the down payment for a home on weed in my lifetime.

I was fifteen the first time I smoked, but I was approaching my sixteenth birthday the first time I got truly stoned. I smoked weed with three friends in a tent in my backyard in what's called a hot box. A term originally reserved for the old tiny solitary confinement cells that would be placed under the heat in southern US prisons, it was later co-opted by weed enthusiasts to mean getting high in a confined space where the feel-good smoke can't escape. Thus getting you higher. A lot higher. I can't remember how much we smoked, but it was enough to make me into an incomprehensible pile of laughing mush. I remember making everyone laugh really hard with an impression of my friend's mom that consisted of me taking my pants off and absolutely nothing else. In retrospect, that's still a brilliant piece of comedy.

Like the dumb teenagers we were, we didn't realize how much we smelled like weed smoke as we went back inside my mother's house. It was like robbing a bank and hiding out in the police station. We were masked men holding sacks with dollar signs on them, giggling in the evidence room and eating Goldfish crackers.

Of course this was the night the police came home early. I heard the door slam shut, and then my mom yelled my name with the same intensity of a movie detective wailing the name of a partner freshly gunned down by the Triads. My friends and I ran upstairs to the bathroom and locked the door (the *perfect* crime!). My mom went back to her training as a customs agent and let us sweat it out in that bathroom for several hours. Maybe it was five minutes; I couldn't really tell. Then, calmly, she called upstairs and said the words you never want to hear your mom say ever, let alone when you're as high as Afroman: "I know what's going on." That night I learned a valuable lesson about smoking pot: don't go back in the house after.

I smoked weed every single day from the age of seventeen to the age of twenty-nine. Most of those years it was all day every day. I compromised my safety and freedom for weed throughout my life. While it was still illegal in Canada, I was pulled over with friends smoking joints in the car three times. One of those times we had just run a stop sign after an illegal U-turn. I was busted green-handed by police officers on more than a few occasions. I was also the worst weed dealer of all time. I would grab a half pound and smoke most of it myself. On more than one occasion I had enough weed on me to send me to jail for years while having conversations with police officers about a different infraction I had just committed (running drunkenly across a buses-only zone, smoking in a non-smoking area, public urination, drinking in public—the usual).

Scariest of all was when Nick from Absolute Comedy and I were in Las Vegas in 2011. We were walking down the Strip at two a.m., drunkenly screaming about how we needed to find weed (even though I had some already, but I wanted more), and our prayers were answered by a dozen men. Now, I've grabbed drugs off a plethora of shady characters in my life. Those people would be scared of the group that encircled us.

"Okay, great, I'll take some, then," I said, hoping these wouldn't be my last words.

"All right, but I can't just give it to you on the street here 'cause of the cops. We gotta go over there." The terrifying man was pointing at a horrifying alley off the Strip that was in complete darkness.

I saw a convenience store on the other side of the alley and had the smartest thought of my life. "The weed is really good?" I said.

"Yeah, yeah, let's go," he said, pointing to the dark alcove, which I now noticed did in fact have a bright neon sign above it reading, *Murder Alley: Now Eleven Seconds without a Shooting!*

"Then I want five hundred dollars' worth. I'm going to go take money out from the bank machine in that convenience store," I said, and then immediately grabbed Nick's hand and made a beeline for the store while the guy tried to explain that there was an ATM for all my shopping needs in Murder Alley. We got to the store and went out the back door, ran a few blocks, and got back on the Strip.

The scariest part hasn't happened yet.

I make the same mistakes a lot. This time, I set a land speed record for the time between making the same mistake twice. We were only two blocks away from the scene of our almost-homicide as a result of yelling about needing weed before we started yelling about needing weed again. The same group of guys caught back up to us.

Suddenly, that moment was the first, only, and I hope last time someone yells at me with a gun in their hand. "Freeze!"

Only cops talk that way. If they'd been wise guys, I wouldn't have heard a thing. I would've been dead.

Will this honesty thing never leave me alone? Okay, I totally stole that line from *Goodfellas*. I'm just trying to sound cool because in reality I was paralyzed with fright. I had weed and cocaine on me, and an armed security guard was pointing his gun at Nick and me, as well as at the guys who were about to rob us, or worse.

"Hands on your head!" he barked.

Nick and I put our hands on our heads, wondering what the buffet was like in Las Vegas jail.

"Get down on the ground!" yelled the guy who for sure tells women he's trying to pick up that he "totally gets to carry a gun and everything."

As we lowered ourselves to the cement, he looked directly at Nick and me. "You two."

Gulp.

His tone changed to a combination of ridicule, shame, and condescension. "Get the fuck outta here. You serious?"

I was pretty close to just going right ahead and calling this book *Whiskey, Weed, and White Privilege: My Life in Bars Instead of behind Them.*

I risked my life three times in under ten minutes for weed that night. When I wasn't risking my life for weed I was wasting it. I used to smoke all day, imagining working for *Saturday Night Live* instead of actually writing. Some of those days I didn't even bother day-dreaming about SNL—I just smoked even more weed instead. It was never far from my thoughts or my lungs.

But I was five days off weed when I recorded episode two of my podcast:

"I just want to experience something not being high. I've always felt like I can't go anywhere or do anything without weed. I always used to think, 'Well, you know, what if I went to the pyramids in Egypt or the Louvre in France or something like that, how could I even do it without weed? How could I experience it?' Which I can only imagine the international incidents that could have arisen from those situations. 'High Man Gets Dorito Dust on the *Mona Lisa*' 'Pothead Asks Pope If He's Down with O.P.P.' So five days off weed— not feeling great, but hopefully I'll feel better soon. Let's get to this episode's interview."

There was only one person who could be my first guest on the podcast. A lot had gone on with Marito since we were first hitting those recovery meetings just over a year earlier. He'd been offered his first nationally televised stand-up set and become one of the hottest names in Canadian comedy. That's why it seemed so weird when he relapsed. About a month before the festival where he would perform his TV set, he was performing at another comedy festival where he got drunk and took a swing at the organizer of the event.

Marito lost his TV taping and went to rehab. I was angry at him. I was hurt for him. Why didn't he just fucking call me first? Is this how I've been making people feel?

He said, "Man, I'll be honest. Alcohol did clear up a lot of like anxieties, fears, like just demons I've had inside of me. But when I was in treatment—and I'm still going through treatment, I still go to therapy, I still go to aftercare, I still go to all that stuff—I just basically like got down to some root traumas that I had in my life. And people like me, they drink because they've formed a habit. It's just all these things that you feel in the present day, but really you're fucking reliving a trauma that you experienced as a kid. Do you know what I'm saying?"

I knew all too well what he was saying.

Before the end of the interview Marito told me how he got sober. "I legitimately treat my condition like diabetes. It's something that I have to constantly check. I go to my counsellors; I go to meetings once a week. I talk to my sponsor. I treat it like something that I take medicine for. But the medicine, for me, is spirituality and talking and being real with myself. Meditating, you know, that's where my medicine is, man. Honestly. But having said that, I also balance it.

"I started realizing that AA, all these things I was carrying, trying to stay sober, I was carrying recovery with me. But now recovery is just like I go into the cabinet once in a while and take my dose, and then I go out into the world."

The best health care is preventative. It's easy to take that medicine when you feel sick. The key is to take that medicine before it happens. That's something addicts struggle with. I know I have.

I was two weeks off pot when I almost cracked. I had made it through the physical withdrawal of quitting weed: a few days of insomnia and not eating. The thing with weed is the mental hold. The fact that it is far and away less harmful than alcohol or hard drugs makes the justifications easier, too. When you know you're whole life won't fall apart from this one joint, it can be tough to abstain. I was trying to edit the episode I had recorded with Marito, but I just couldn't get it right. I was getting angry at my favourite punching bag—myself. I couldn't focus, and I started making the usual justifications.

I can't do this podcast all by myself. I'll find a producer or network that wants it, and then I only have to worry about the recording. While I'm waiting for that to happen, I might as well start smoking weed again. Okay, let's put a pin in the podcast thing until I get my shit together.

Those are the kinds of thoughts you have to constantly out-think as an addict. The addict voice in my head is persistent, persuasive, and pervasive. In my experience that voice can dish out a ton of punishment—it's a bully. In boxing there's one way you can stop a bully dead in its tracks: punch it right in the fucking mouth.

Get my shit together by running back to weed? Quitting weed was how I was getting my shit together! I thought about all the half-finished scripts, never-started projects, and times that I had stared at a blank computer screen in frustration, only to give up and choose the safe confines of altering my brain. I worked harder at drugs than I did at comedy. Those were the thoughts I used to motivate myself. But I already knew I was motivated enough to do this podcast; the question was, was I disciplined enough? I gave it another couple hours and inched my way to finishing the episode.

By now, I had three episodes recorded and edited. I had my podcast cover photo, and I was approved by all the major audio platforms. There was only one thing left to do: release the episodes. I didn't know what my friends and family would think. There were so many people close to me who didn't know about what I had been through. So I wrote a Facebook status and attached a link to my podcast.

It's been 797 days since I last did cocaine.

It's been 489 days since my last drink.

It's been 24 days since I last smoked weed.

I have a new podcast where I'm quitting WEED, CAFFEINE, CHEWING MY NAILS, RED MEAT, DAIRY, CIGARETTES, PORN, SOCIAL MEDIA, CREDIT CARDS, GOSSIP, SMARTPHONES, SUGAR … This is an insanely personal project and I'm already instantly regretting it for a variety of reasons. AA meetings aren't for me, so I'm doing this podcast instead.

Less than twenty-four hours after posting the first three episodes I started getting messages on social media from people telling me about their struggles with addiction and thanking me for the podcast. Lots of people messaged me: strangers, acquaintances I hadn't talked to in years, family, casual friends, best friends, and most important of all, Nora.

chapter 9

caffeine

I was in grade twelve when I had my first cup of coffee, second cup of coffee, and third cup of coffee. If you've read this far, you might be able to guess that those were all in a row. It would be another year before I could even touch the stuff again because of how awful my stomach, nerves, and tongue felt after shotgunning three coffees for the first time. My fourth cup came when I was so wretchedly hungover one morning I didn't think I'd be able to make it to class that day. The magical elixir shot me from my hangover right into class, where I felt re-energized and refocused—and fell asleep fifteen minutes later. I stopped going to my classes but kept drinking coffee. After all, if you're going to smoke weed all day, you're going to need a pick-me-up every now and again and again and again and again.

Coffee helped me live my unhealthy, some might say depraved, lifestyle over the next ten years. It could turn me from a half-drunk, barely slept, slurring zombie into that same thing but with enough energy to be able to make it through the non-alcohol-drinking/non-hard-drug-using hours of the day.

Over the years, I was able to stop drinking coffee for a couple of months at a time every now and then, before restarting my caffeine cycle. It always went like this: Have a coffee—Have a lot of coffee for months—Have so much coffee it makes me sick—Quit—Go a few months without—Convince myself I no longer have a problem—Make justifications—Have a coffee. I don't want to disparage coffee too much. Much like its dumber sibling marijuana, it has proven health benefits. But like weed, I abused it to the point where I didn't reap those benefits. I also don't want to be confronted outside of bookstores by an angry torch-wielding mob of people who share cute coffee memes like:

Eat. Sleep. Coffee. Repeat.

Don't talk to me 'til I've had my coffee!

I will stab you in the face until I get coffee.

My first cup of the day was always an extra large with a double shot of espresso, which I would chase with several more cups throughout the day. All without water or food, just coffee and cigarettes. Some days I would push it too far, and believe me, I'm speaking from experience when I say being coffee sick isn't that far from being dope sick. Your heart is beating off rhythm, and you're sweating and feeling nauseated and ineffectual. The good news is that, like cocaine, caffeine doesn't stay in your system that long. It makes sense that, even in their cellular forms, cocaine and coffee can't wait to get moving. They just fly around in your bloodstream screaming, "This is boring! Let's get the fuck out of here and *do* something!"

My years of drinking acidic hot liquid on an empty stomach that was already damaged from dairy it couldn't handle had caught up to me with the ulcers I'd been diagnosed with the previous year. After my first shot at the quit list fell through, I was back to my old ways with coffee, and I hit the point where I always know I'm in trouble with a substance: I can't feel anything or do anything unless I have it in my system. The one good thing about quitting caffeine is that the withdrawal symptoms and most intense cravings only last about a week for me. Don't get it twisted; it's a godforsaken week that sees me almost strike a child. But it's only a week.

It was time to quit caffeine, again.

During this time, the shaking hands and body tremors were ramping up in frequency and ferocity. I was even falling to the ground on a regular basis now. I'm aware that for such a scary problem I've been withholding a lot of details from you, reader. But there's a lot of scary shit I'm just not ready to tell you.

• • •

Nora was a new comedian on the scene who I remembered seeing perform only once before, eight months earlier, at an open mic in a dive bar for next to no audience. Usually, those are the kind of circumstances that let you forget someone, but Nora was unforgettable. Her voice sounded like if a valley girl taught constitutional law at Harvard. She stood out as uniquely funny in a comedy scene of 4,000 people. All I said to her that night was "Good set," and then I was disappointed when I didn't see her around at shows after that. So I was pleasantly surprised when, the day after I launched my podcast, she sent me a message that read, *Yo, Alex, I just listened to the first episode of your podcast. It's fucking amazing. I'm an ex(ish) addict. That was very compelling to listen to. Really cool.*

I wished her luck on her recovery and mentioned that maybe she could come on the podcast sometime. Later that night we happened to be on the same comedy show. It wasn't just the leather jacket and charming winks that made me think she was perhaps the coolest person I'd ever met. Nora carried herself like the world is something of an imposition that she wryly tolerates. What takes me hundreds of words and lots of yelling to make funny, Nora did with four words and a subtle eyebrow raise. I know this is the oldest line said by men with popped collars and dropped trousers, but she had the most beautiful blue eyes. Not the serial-killer kind, either—you know, the ones where there is nothing behind them but the memories of the last screams of their victims. Nora's eyes were warm and expressive. She didn't take herself too seriously, but I sure did.

After the show we were sitting on the curb and I already knew I liked her when I flicked my cigarette to the gutter, took a deep breath, and said, "Okay, tonight is the night a beautiful sober girl comes up to me and we end up together."

I didn't know if she knew I was hoping it was her. We went into the corner store and I got her a ChapStick and laughed loudly when she said this was just like the movie *Pretty Woman*. She said she would have to buy me a peppermint tea sometime to make it up to me. For the first time in my life I didn't even care if she only wanted to be my friend; I just knew I wanted to be around her again.

She messaged me again at two a.m. that night. *Nice to see ya, thanks for the ChapStick. I owe you a peppermint tea.*

You most certainly do. Once I know a girl likes me, I try to say as few words as possible so as to not fuck it up.

Hold me to it. Or I owe you my first-born child.

So I get a tea or the privilege of being a single father?

Yeah, I mean, I'll help out a little. Like I'll throw you a baby shower. But that's it. Let me know what you choose. The tea I can get to you in the next week. The baby might take a bit longer. Like six months. Really depends how good you want the baby to be.

That line is the most hilarious foreshadowing you'll ever hear.

We made a date for Sunday night, which was also my last day having caffeine. In comedy, timing is everything.

Nora and I were meeting at an Indian spot. We ordered colas because I was five hours away from quitting caffeine. Then I spilled the lentils and confessed that it was my first time at an Indian restaurant, which Nora responded to by telling me about her three months in India, one of those months spent alone. I found out she had travelled all over the world. Nora found out the foreign destinations I'd been to: Las Vegas, Baltimore, and Las Vegas again.

Skin deep we were different, but down to the bone we were the same. She'd been a comedy nerd her whole life, and we shared the same values, gifts, and curses. Nora knew addiction and had lost one of her best friends to an overdose a few months earlier. She was raised Jewish and I grew up Catholic, so we were both brought up to call our mother's when we got there. No matter where there happened to be.

We were both so honest about our pasts, things were flowing so naturally, and the whole thing was so non-judgmental that it didn't feel like a date. We frequently changed gears between laughs from our bellies and words from our hearts. Before I'd even finished my meal, I knew I wanted to have tandoori chicken with Nora again.

After dinner we went for coffees and drank them in the park as the sun went down. I was chain-smoking because I had to get as many coffee-and-cigarette combos into me as possible before midnight. I had my last coffee at about 9:30 and two cigarettes in a row before I asked Nora if she wanted to go back to my place.

We had made an agreement to not engage in sexual congress; we didn't want to spoil such a spiritually fulfilling evening with our most carnal of desires. But the kissing from the living room flowed into my bedroom, and our clothes were falling faster than my blood pressure was rising from all the caffeine. Our connection ran deeper after only four hours than I had previously thought was possible. Feelings simply overtook us as we kissed deeply with a passion that belied the short time we'd spent in one another's company. Lying vulnerable and naked beside each other on the bed, we began the delicate process of knowing another human being in that most intimate of ways.

But yo, my dick was soft.

"Straight up, this never happens to me. It must have been all the coffee and cigarettes." This was my actual penis talking.

All the unwanted erections of my youth came flooding—well, not *flooding*—back to me in my mind at once. I wanted to reach out to one of those memories, grab it tight, and put it into my pants. But alas, the ghost-boners of yore were just that: ghost-boners.

Why was this happening? I'm not a penis scientist, but I have theories. Before this point in my life, I had never had sex without weed or alcohol in my system. Even with long-term partners. Like a lot of things, it was too scary sober. Of all the things I had figured out I could do without booze or drugs, it turned out sex wasn't one of them. I believed Nora when she said she didn't care, but I still wanted to run out to buy weed. Her being okay with me not being able to have sex with her just made me want to have sex with her even more. Nora's honesty, compassion, and heart gave me something that was rare in my life. Certainly rare for how brief a time I'd known her. I didn't even know what to call it because I'd only ever heard about it. Is this what trust is?

Which led to us having sex later that night. Twice. So there. Where's your childish joke about my last name being Wood now?

It was the kind of first date you see in a rom-com so cheesy you shit in your own hand just so you have something to throw at the screen. We stayed up until five a.m. and told each other our deepest secrets and favourite song lyrics. Just before the birds started mocking anyone leaving a party, Nora fell asleep beside me in my bed. In the previous 500 or so days, I'd had a lot of sleepless nights staring up at the ceiling, trying to figure out how I could have gotten it so wrong. That night, I wondered how I could have gotten it so right.

• • •

A few hours after Nora left the next day, Meg came over to record episode five of the podcast. I first met Meg when I was on one those East Coast benders/comedy tours. Some of my favourite wrestlers growing up were always introduced as being from "parts unknown." It always sounded ominous, like this person was so different that the place they were from wasn't even known to humans. Meg's uniqueness is such that if you ever ended up in parts unknown and asked if anyone knew her, they would reply, "You mean President Meg?"

She has a wondrously strange mind and warm heart. Meg and I had been through the wringer together; we'd performed together in everything from roast battles to rap battles and were fucked up for most of it. Little did I know that when I was sneaking off to do cocaine, she had been sneaking off to do amphetamines. She was barely a month off the shit when she came on the podcast.

Before the end of the interview, Meg made me feel like I was doing the right thing when she said, "I've known you for a long time. You just are a way better person sober. It's not like you were ever shitty or whatever. It's more like you're a whole wonderful human being and not just like the spark of what's inside you that I loved when I first met you. Now that's you all the time rather that just sometimes."

Even if it ended in an hours-long splitting withdrawal headache, it was hard not to feel good about day one off caffeine after the interview with Meg.

• • •

Day two was a little harder. As I was walking to a show, I got the urge for a peppermint tea. I walked into a coffee shop downtown where I was puzzled to see a completely empty café. Finally, I noticed one of the coffee shop employees knocking on the washroom door while saying, "Sir, you've been in there over forty minutes. Legally, we have to open the door."

That's for sure not a law. I've done zero days of law school, and even I know there isn't a law that's says the shit you're taking is so massive it's illegal. I'd be on death row if that were true.

Still, the employee tried to open the door with a key—but the door was jammed shut. She looked through the crack, and then quickly turned and said to me and the empty chairs, "Someone call 9-1-1."

Being the only someone there, I took out my phone and dialed the number, while walking towards the bathroom. If you've never opened a door that's blocked with the body of an incapacitated person let me just tell you, there's an art to it. You have to use enough force to open the door with all of that dead weight against it but not so much as to injure the person. It was a tricky task for someone who was more used to being the one on the other side of the door. I got it open to see a guy passed out on the floor with a bag of coke, a vial of crack, and a vial of heroin beside him. I came into this coffee shop expecting to fight the temptation to drink coffee, and instead, it was like Christmas morning and my brother was still sleeping—all the presents could be mine. It's shameful to admit what my first thought was.

Here's a list of what my first thought *wasn't*:

Is this guy alive?

Be careful.

Stay calm so you can tell 9-1-1 what's happening.

No, the first thought that ran through my head was:

Take the coke.

It was even in Tony Montana's voice.

"9-1-1. What's your emergency?"

"I'm at a coffee shop at Queen and Bathurst. There's a drug overdose."

"We're sending someone immediately. Why do you think it's a drug overdose?"

"'Cause this guy is passed out in the bathroom and there are drugs everywhere."

"Is he breathing normally?"

"I think so."

"Tell me every time he breathes."

"Okay ... He breathed ... He breathed ... He breathed ..." After that, I stopped, because I thought she just wanted to know the rate of his breathing. Never assume.

"Oh my God, did he stop breathing?"

"Nah, nah, he's still breathing."

"I told you to tell me every time he breathes," she snapped. I feel like the operator and I were trapped in a loveless marriage.

"He breathed."

"Okay, now if he vomits in his mouth—"

"He breathed."

"I'm going to need you to go ahead—"

"He breathed."

"And use your finger to clear the vomit out of his mouth so he doesn't choke."

And now, the next thought to go through my head was:

Well, I guess this guy is going to die if he vomits.

Finally, a firefighter arrived on the scene. He walked confidently to the bathroom, gave me a thumbs-up, and then leaned down to the passed-out guy and said in a thick Canadian accent, "How ya feelin' there, bahd?"

I left as the man on the bathroom floor started to regain consciousness. I was dismayed when, after all that, the place still charged me for my peppermint tea. Drinking my hot minty tonic while walking through downtown Toronto, all I could think was *That could have been me.*

One week later I was off to New York City for the first time in my life.

• • •

Simon and Garfunkel are liars; there is nothing romantic about a twelve-hour Greyhound bus ride through America. Yeah, I was looking for America, too, but it was harder when the guy sitting beside me smelled like a pile of garbage that a group of skunks had sex on top of. Garbage-skunk-orgy smell or not, I was still happy, though, because it took me a long time to get on this bus. New York City has always been my favourite place I've never been to. In my youth I would see pictures of the Ramones, the Strokes, or Jay-Z with NYC in the background and it filled my head with dreams of being a part of that city. But like a lot of my dreams, I put them on hold so I could get drunk and high instead. That wasn't me anymore. Damn copyright laws prevent me from using song lyrics in this book, so I'll have to paraphrase: Begin sharing the news, I'm departing today. Arriving roughly midday tomorrow.

The bus drove through the darkness of the Lincoln Tunnel and made it to the light at the other end. Picture what we've all seen in a million movies a million times: You know the helicopter shot that sweeps across the whole city? Then it's just hard cuts to: Times Square, a line of traffic with hundreds of yellow taxis, Broadway, Madison Square Garden, crowded sidewalks, Central Park, steam coming out of the sewers, pizza places, the Empire State Building. And then the camera goes back to a wide aerial shot of the city so nice they named it twice. Well, that's what I saw, but through the window of a Greyhound bus.

I got off in the heart of Times Square, which was pulsating rapidly and overwhelmingly, as if on cocaine. I live in the fourth-biggest city in North America, but this was all way too much. I was frozen with fear, chain-smoking. I couldn't figure out which subway train would take me to where I was staying in Brooklyn. My back was literally against the wall and people were still bumping into me. I felt like I was going to have a panic attack.

Why was I such a little boy? Relapse starts with those thoughts, and those thoughts lead to other thoughts.

"I need you to come pick me up at the bar. I'm too drunk to get to your house," I admit in shame over the phone.

My friend sighs and asks where I am. I'm so drunk so quick that I'm blurring and slurring when I tell her the name of the place. I made it through so much already without relapsing on booze, and it took New York City less than ten minutes to put me down. I chose the easy way out and went to the bar. I'm staring into my beer, but I don't want to be this guy anymore.

Well, I'm not—because this didn't happen. I had two choices. Doing what I imagined happening when I played the tape out, or doing what I came here to do. Forty minutes later, I was in Brooklyn.

Gleason's is one of the most famous boxing gyms in the world. It started in the Bronx but ended up in Brooklyn under the Manhattan Bridge. Ali, Durán, LaMotta, Tyson, Hearns, Holmes, and now Wood had all thrown punches in this gym. I walked there, taking in the sights and famous street names I had heard in hip hop songs my whole life. A trainer saw me working on the bag and told me I had decent power. We talked a bit more in the locker room, after I finished surpassing the ghosts of boxing past.

"How many fights you had?" he asked while peeling an orange.

"*O* and *O*," I say, wildly excited because I was shocked he thought it was possible I'd had a couple amateur fights.

"You have zero fights? Damn, kid, what are you waiting for?" A clean bill of health, I didn't tell him.

We talked about our favourite fights and fighters, but before I left he noticed something in my gym bag.

"Can't be a smoker in this sport," he said, glancing at the pack of cigarettes.

"I'm quitting soon."

"Good. Those things will take your heart away, and trust me, you need heart for this shit."

For a second, it seemed like he was placed in this gym for me by a higher power. Then, he said, "You should drink coffee. Coffee is a stimulant. Go with that."

That night, I took the subway from Brooklyn into Manhattan to do what I came here to do: comedy. I had spent the last ten years of my career watching other comedians come here for shows. I would see them talking about it online, and it would fill me with bitterness: *That's supposed to be me.* I wouldn't do anything about it, though; I would just sulk at the bar. If you remove the booze from that situation, I was just sulking. There's only so much sulking you can do stone cold sober before you say to yourself, "Why don't I actually do something about this instead of, y'know ... *sulking*?"

I also had work to do. My close friend Jhanelle, who had moved to NYC to go to NYU, was letting me stay with her in Brooklyn. Jhanelle used to stay on my couch sometimes, and we would talk late into the night about Kanye West, our families, comedy, and the world. Jhanelle can sing, rap, dance, act, listen, talk, and do comedy. Her heart is fully functional despite being made of gold. We had gotten drunk together in the past, but Jhanelle was really only addicted to one thing: coffee. She was eight months off of it when we sat down to record her interview for my podcast.

Jhanelle said something that could have been me talking about cocaine, booze, weed, coffee or anything else. "The thing that I loved the most about coffee was that like I felt like the person that I wanted to be."

I related to this as much as anything that had been said on my podcast. It's like I keep expecting something to complete me. I felt like I wasn't finished, but I wanted to be.

Jhanelle and I were booked to do a comedy storytelling show in Queens. Before the gig we went down to the water to look across the river at the city. The sun was setting over the most famous skyline in the world, and as it got lower, the buildings masked it, creating a cascade of hundreds of sunbeams pouring through the cracks between them. The only thing more captivating was when we went back to the same spot after the show and saw it again, at night, with all the sparkling lights. I felt a strange sense of longing while staring out, though—like I wasn't experiencing it fully. And that weed would make it better. Or a coffee would make it better. I tried an ice cream, to at least feel something while I stared, but that didn't help. I couldn't put my finger on exactly why, but something was missing. Then I started to think that maybe I was wrong and I was experiencing it more because I was sober.

That week I trained at Gleason's like I was fighting Ken Norton at Yankee Stadium on Saturday night and performed comedy all across the city. It was the week in New York that I'd always wanted. I have only a few regrets of things I didn't get to do:

- Smack the roof of a cab and yell, "I'm walkin' here!"
- Strut down the street oozing seventies sexuality to the Bee Gees's "Stayin' Alive."
- Make friends with a pigeon lady in Central Park before she helped me thwart two bad guys with a series of booby traps.
- Use my world-renowned karate skills to take down an international crime syndicate in the Bronx.
- Scream, "Attica!" over and over again.
- Meet a frog, piggy, bear, and some sort of weird blue creature and help them "take" Manhattan.

- Scale the Empire State Building in the clutches of a gigantic prehistoric ape.

Leaving Times Square on the bus I told myself, *I have to make it back here one day.*

• • •

When I got home I had an interview with the *Toronto Star* for an article about my podcast. It was my first appearance in a major newspaper since the *Montreal Gazette* wrote about me at Just for Laughs eight years before. My inboxes were flooded with people who had discovered my podcast, thanking me for helping to inspire them.

I had been doing the podcast for less than two months, but I'd already gone longer without weed than ever before. It's not that I didn't want it so much as I didn't even think about it. Same with caffeine.

Oh yeah, I hope you didn't forget about Nora because I sure didn't. Other than the night after our first date and when I was in NYC, we'd spent every single day together. I was vulnerable with her in ways I hadn't been with anyone, and she was with me. We talked until dawn, laughed until it hurt, and kissed until it didn't. It was the best physical and emotional connection I'd ever had with someone. Nora didn't make me feel lucky to be with her. That might sound unromantic, but I always felt lucky to be with any woman. Nora made me feel like we were both lucky. I liked myself through her eyes. We were making the classic errors of dating another addict and moving too fast, but we didn't care.

I knew we had something really special one night when I fell to the ground and couldn't get up because of leg tremors. I told her to leave. She wouldn't, so I started to get angry. I didn't want anyone to see me like this.

She lay down beside me on the floor and said, "I'm not going anywhere. If you can't get up, we'll just lie here for a while."

There was only one problem: Nora was a recovering heroin and opioid addict who was still doing something called kratom every day. Kratom is a plant that mimics the effects of an opioid. The jury is still out about whether addicts should use it as an alternative to opioids, similar to methadone. Some users swear it got them off heroin, but there's also research suggesting that it's like jumping from the frying pan into the fryer.

I wanted to make this relationship work, but I knew that I had to put my recovery first. It was a conversation both of us were putting off, but it had to happen sometime. It was around date 10 or 210 (it was hard to tell because I felt like I'd always known her) that she asked me if I'd be able to date her considering she still did kratom.

"So, you're doing it ... every day?" I asked.

"Yeah, but it's herbal. It doesn't cause the same damage heroin does. Opioid addicts are swearing by it. It's like a natural-growing methadone."

I hadn't played games or hidden anything from this woman, but I had to test her on something.

"Can I have some?"

"What?"

"Can I have some kratom?"

"What do you mean?"

"You're saying it's so great, it's herbal. It's not on my list of things to quit."

"I get what you're doing. I get it."

"Do you?"

Nora put her head down and there was a long pause. "Are you going to be able to be with me?"

"I don't care if you relapse every week. I don't care if you go into withdrawal and turn into a complete monster for a while. But if you don't at least try, if you just decide that the kratom life is for you, then no, I can't be with you. I just can't."

"It's not like I don't want to quit. I want to quit, and not just so I can be with you. I want to do it for myself."

That was all I needed to hear.

• • •

"What magical destination will you whisk us away to next, oh humble, well-endowed narrator?"

I'm glad you asked, because what happens next is the happiest, purest feeling of joy a human being can experience. And there's only one place on earth that can be the backdrop for a feeling like that: Buffalo. They say that Vermont is for lovers, but the man masturbating in the Buffalo Taco Bell would beg to differ.

Towards the end of April I was headlining a comedy club in Buffalo; this would be my first time closing a show outside Canada. There's a big difference between a pro show and the open mics I'd seen Nora perform at. She was a powerhouse comedian in the making, but still in the making. Nora had bombed when she'd opened for me at the last show I'd headlined a week before, and I knew she was too new and raw for pro shows, but I wanted to give her one more shot. I obviously didn't tell her, but if this one didn't go well, I would have to stop vouching for her to open pro shows for a while, until she was ready. I had done it because she was just so funny I knew it was only a matter of time before I would be the one opening for her. Fine, I also didn't want to be away from her for even one night.

On the drive to Buffalo, I told Nora about a character I do called Unshakable Radio DJ Who Always Throws to Eddie Money. No matter what horrible news story he has to read on the air, he never breaks out of the upbeat radio-DJ voice and always plays an Eddie Money song afterwards.

All right, got a traffic update for those of you on the 401. There's a thirty-five-car pileup and dozens have been decapitated. Speaking of that, get ready to lose your head for Eddie Money's "Two Tickets to Paradise!"

Or

Little news for ya on the morning drive. Russia has dropped nukes across the world and those who weren't lucky enough to die in the initial blast are having the skin peel from their faces. Here's another real face-melter. It's "Take Me Home Tonight" by Eddie Money.

That night I threw Nora to the lions and she came out wearing a lion's head for a hat. She was wonderful onstage: loose, present, and just in the pocket. Then I went up and murdered for nearly an hour; it was one of the best headlining sets I'd ever had. Nora and I got back into the car for the drive back to Toronto feeling like the top of the world was just the floor below us that kept complaining about the party we were having upstairs. Nora had barely ever performed out-side of her hometown, I had only performed in the States a handful of times, let alone headlined, and we both came out looking pretty. They couldn't even lay a glove on us that night.

I thought we had already covered our entire beings, so it felt surprising that we hadn't talked about him until that drive home.

"What are your thoughts on Bruce Springsteen?" Nora asked.

"I would die for him," I said.

"Me too. Like, I would let you die for him," she said, before putting on one of the best songs ever recorded. We drove down a dark high-way, illuminated only by headlights, "Born to Run" blaring.

We belted out with our combined nine-out-of-ten singing voices—six for Nora, three for me. After the first chorus, I stopped singing and just watched her belt her heart out. She was pounding on the steering wheel during the drum fills, her hair wildly dancing every which way, with so much emotion in her voice I could tell she was really feeling it.

In the days before this trip I was pushing the thought away when it would come into my brain. *It's too soon. It's not possible in less than a month, no matter how many hours you've spent together. Life isn't a romantic comedy. That's not how it works. This is the pink cloud talking. You can't know someone well enough in only a few weeks to truly feel that word, so don't say it. If anything, you thinking this is just proof that you don't even know what it means.*

But even before the Boss could yell out, "One, two, three, four" before the last chorus, I was more sure of it than I'd ever been sure of anything. *I'm in love with Nora.*

Then she motioned with her hand for me to start singing with her again. The people we had lost. The addictions that had kicked the shit out of us. The substances we both still had to quit and the challenges that would come with that. Our broken hearts and busted dreams. The love that we felt in our hearts but had not yet spoken aloud to each other. It all came out in that last chorus. That beautiful copyrighted chorus that I don't have the resources to include the lyrics to here.

There in the darkness on the edge of town I was happier than I'd ever been. But that's when old habits come out. *Don't be this happy. Something bad is going to happen. Something bad always happens. You aren't allowed to be happy. You're cursed. You're gonna curse this girl. You're setting yourself up to get your heart ripped out here. She's going to see you're not good enough. Someone or something is going to take this from you. You might as well fuck it up on purpose before you fuck it up by accident. At least that way you control the fuck-up. Something bad is going to happen.*

No. I remembered that I controlled my life. Nothing bad was going to happen.

And then, something bad happened.

As soon as we got in the door from Buffalo we couldn't keep our hands off each other. But while Nora was on top of me, she said the most alarming thing a person can hear during sex: "Oh my God, don't look down." As she said it, she demanded I cover my eyes with my hands.

"What's wrong?"

"Just promise me you won't look down."

It was like the worst surprise party in history.

"What the fuck?" she whispered like she was staring at a ghost.

"Nora, what's going on? I'm gonna open my eyes, okay?"

Once, I saw a buddy of mine get hit with a baseball bat in a street fight. When we were kids I locked my brother out of the house, and since we were raised on nineties action movies, he tried to get back inside by punching a hole in a window and it sliced his arm open. I've watched professional and amateur boxing for longer than I can even remember. I'd still never seen this much blood in my life. I immediately ran to the bathroom door, behind which Nora had closed herself.

"Are you okay?"

"Yeah, it's just my period is really heavy and it won't stop."

I'm far from an expert on the subject. In fact, it wasn't until I was of voting age that I found out that the moon is somehow involved in the menstrual cycle. But even I knew this couldn't be her period.

"Can I come in?"

"No. I'll clean everything up. Just give me a couple minutes."

Twenty minutes later, we called a cab and put a towel down in the back seat. Nora and I were the only people in the emergency room laughing as we waited to get called in.

"That's probably going to be a one-star passenger rating," she said.

Around two a.m. they told us that Nora had suffered a miscarriage. She fell asleep for a couple of minutes and I went outside, chain-smoked, and called my sister. When I came back Nora was awake and about to get an ultrasound.

"Why?" I asked.

"To give us one of those cute miscarriage ultrasound pictures to hang on the fridge," Nora said before asking, "How did I even get pregnant? I thought I did enough drugs to make me infertile. That's always been my birth control plan."

"This is the worst first date I've ever been on," I said.

"Because of that you're going to leave me to raise a bloody bed-sheet alone?"

We kept ratcheting up the inappropriate comments until I joked, "I think this guy can hear us," thinking the ultrasound technician would finally laugh.

He just stared me dead in the eyes and nodded.

Nora kept bleeding throughout the night and into the morning. At around eight a.m., she had a cervical exam. Nora'd had a cervical ectopic pregnancy.

"I think it means there's a dinosaur growing inside of you." We were on fire.

A worried doctor came in and told us this was an emergency situation and Nora would have to be rushed to another hospital. Things started being less funny, and no one was giving us all the information. It's scary when you're in an emergency room and put on a stretcher and led to an ambulance to be taken to another emergency room because your specific emergency is such an emergency that it can't be handled in that emergency room. Nora started to look scared in the ambulance, and she reached out for my hand. She looked up into my eyes, and I knew she needed to hear something comforting.

"All right, drivers, be careful on the streets of Toronto today because there is an ambulance driving wildly. We got a miscarriage in the back, and we're losing a lot of blood. For the ride over to the next hospital we got Eddie Money with 'Baby Hold on to Me.'"

"More like 'Baby Don't Hold on to Me.'" She'd lost blood but not her wit.

Nora was in her fourth hospital bed, in her second hospital, when the seventh doctor we'd seen that morning walked in to fully explain the situation. The zygote was growing outside of the uterus in an ectopic pregnancy, in this case in the cervix. It was quite dangerous and there was a host of potential complications. Nora had lost a lot of blood and was going to need a transfusion and an embolization to stop the bleeding.

"The craziest part is cervical ectopic miscarriages are one in a million and we just had one last week. What are the odds?" the doctor said.

"You want to hear something really crazy? That one was mine, too!" I said, while giving a little air thrust.

The doctor laughed and said, "You're the funniest person I've—" All right, all right, the doctor looked horrified after that joke.

Nora took the brave step of telling her Jewish mother she was in the hospital. Three seconds later a puff of smoke appeared and her mom was there.

Meeting your partner's parents is always awkward, but this situation was a special kind of awkward. What was I supposed to say?

"Hi, I'm Alex. I had unprotected sexual intercourse with your daughter and now my demon seed is trying to kill her. So, Robert, I hear you're quite the golfer."

The doctor wheeled Nora away for the procedure, and now I was sitting with Nora's mom on my right and her dad on my left. We stared forward in silence. After about five minutes I took out a pack of gum and popped a piece in.

"You have gum," Nora's dad said.

"Yes, would you like some?"

"No, thanks."

Long pause.

"Gum's making a bit of a comeback," he said.

I was unaware that gum had gone anywhere that necessitated a comeback, but all things considered, the conversation could have been weirder.

When Nora came out of the embolization she was screaming in agony. "End it," she kept repeating, while sobbing in pain.

They wheeled her into a room and she only wanted to see her mother. When Salma came out she told me that there was nothing more I could do and Nora wanted me to go home. Robert drove me and we talked about the merits of dental gum over bubble gum. Our conversation flowed so naturally that the next logical step was to start a new podcast with Robert about gum called *Just Chewin' It*.

I had been up for well over twenty-four hours by the time I got home, and I didn't even have the energy to wash the blood off my body or my bed. I woke up a few hours later to a text from Nora telling me she had a hospital room. I went to the hospital that night—after showering; I'm not Hannibal Lecter. I changed the sheets, too. In case you're squeamish, there's only, like, seventeen more instances of someone bleeding between now and the end of the book.

At the hospital Nora told me they had given her methotrexate, a kind of chemotherapy. It was the most effective treatment to normalize the levels of her human chorionic gonadotropin, or hCG, for you laypeople. My God, it's like you've never read a book before this one.

We decided that, considering I'd gotten her pregnant and all, we should probably put a label on this thing. I was going to call this book *How to Trap a Beautiful Woman*, but for various reasons the publisher advised me against it. Thanks a lot, PC Police.

At the hospital the next night I met her younger sister, Jennifer, who possesses the same combination of weird and warm as Nora. The three of us laughed inappropriately loudly for a hospital, in a shared room. The only time we weren't laughing was when the chemo was really taking hold or Nora hemorrhaged. Those times I just held her hand and tried to get her to focus on her breathing, which is what I would do whenever I thought I couldn't take any more pain from boxing, comedy, withdrawal, or just life.

"Just keep breathing," I said. "In through your nose, out through your mouth. Just keep breathing."

On the third day, a whole team of doctors came in to talk to us. Even I'd never seen a whole team of doctors in real life before. Television lied to me, though, because I didn't pick up on a single case of a sexy, unspoken "will they, won't they?" vibe coming from any of them. The boring doctors with their disappointing, strictly-professional relationships told us that two doses of the methotrexate was usually enough to lower hCG to the normal level, but it still wasn't working for Nora. They assured us this third dose would be enough, and we'd be out of there the next day.

Those days were long and a coffee would have been nice, but I didn't need one to feel like a complete person.

chapter 10

nail biting

I'm well aware that, on the surface, quitting biting my nails seems like it pales in comparison to quitting drinking and drugs. Nobody has ever gotten pregnant from biting their nails, and if they did, they really needed to wash their hands more thoroughly. I've never heard of someone—after biting their tenth nail off the cuticle—finding the confidence to fight a cop. Neil Young didn't sing about the nail and the damage done. However, nail biting is clinically recognized by the American Psychiatric Association in the *Diagnostic and Statistical Manual of Mental Disorders* as a behaviour under the umbrella of obsessive-compulsive disorder.

Nail biting is my longest-standing vice. Ever since I was able to open my mouth, I've put my fingers in there—which almost saw me name this book *Filters and Fingers: My Life in Oral Fixations*. Orders to "Stop biting your nails" from aunts/teachers/partners/strangers on the bus have persisted for my entire life. I've always wanted to stop, but truth be told, I usually only make it two weeks—until they're fully grown. And then I feel pathologically compelled to chew them again. It is debilitating in social situations. Try chewing your nails in public and not have it look like you're contemplating where to hide the severed head you have lying around at home. I'm constantly self-consciously trying to avoid showing my fingernails to anyone. It's like I'm a horrible magician. "Now, for my next trick—watch me make a phone call with my knuckles!"

I also realize how unhealthy it is. I live in one of the biggest cities in North America, with a subway system that has more than a million daily passengers, yet I'll touch a pole and then bite my nails a few seconds after. If there's ever a pandemic, I'll be a zombie before Brad Pitt can even look into the camera and say, "It's gone global" (I wrote this line in September 2019; I'm so sorry if it awakened an ancient curse).

By now I was able to recognize my triggers to use drugs and alcohol, so I applied that to this bad habit. I noticed right away that a major trigger for nail biting was being hungry. Apparently, I prefer my food al dente. Feeling anxious is what is most commonly associated with biting one's nails, and I definitely recognized that trigger in myself.

But most disturbing of all was the impulse to hurt myself. Apologies again to the squeamish, but I like peeling back the nail when I take almost all of it off and it actually produces blood. The biggest similarity between nail biting and substance abuse for me was knowing how much it would hurt later, how much I'd regret doing it, how bad it was for me, wishing I could quit, and still doing it anyway.

One of the people who runs the comedy show where Nora and I first started talking is a sweet and funny guy named Joel. He's a fellow nail-biter, so I sat down with him to record the tenth episode of my podcast. Right off the bat, Joel confirmed that I'm not the only one who deals with biting their nails on such a deep level.

"It's hard, and people think it's gross and I think it is gross. I was, like, hurting myself. I liked the pain. I miss the pain now. My mom used to just tell me to stop and tell me to stop, and that made me want to do it more. It almost becomes like my thing, you know? It's like, 'Oh, no, this is my thing. I like doing this. This is my thing. Why, why would anyone tell me to stop doing this? Because this is what I do and it's part of who I am.'"

It's times like these when you see why it matters to talk to people about addiction. I was convinced that I was the only person in history who dealt with biting my nails for such complex reasons. It's a heavy burden to carry that much shame and anger around with you everywhere, all the time, all alone. Joel's words gave me such comfort, and I felt my whole body get lighter.

The first day off biting my nails is always a real nail-biter. If you've chosen to stop reading after that sentence, I get it. I couldn't help myself. I sincerely apologize to you and your family for that line. But it is truly an agonizing day. I'm dumbstruck to discover how many times I bring my stupid fingers up to my stupider mouth to chew on my stupider-er nails.

But being in a hospital most of that first day was the best possible place to quit biting my nails. Just thinking about the thousands of communicable diseases that came through those doors every year was enough to make me drop my fingers swiftly every time I subconsciously raised them to my mouth. Most of all, watching Nora handle her brutal situation like a day at the dentist really brought to light how easy it should be for me to quit this habit.

After every unsuccessful chemo treatment the doctors assured us that the next one would work—only to have our hopes dashed. We were falling in love anyway. I would race Nora around the hospital in a wheelchair and we'd end up outside smoking. It really was just like any of our previous twenty or so dates, except Nora was wearing a hospital gown. One time I got in the wheelchair and Nora pushed me, along with her IV bag, because we thought it made a funny visual.

"Faster, faster!" I mock-ordered her as we passed horrified onlookers in the hospital lobby.

Nora ended up getting six doses of chemo and two blood transfusions over the twelve days she was in the hospital for the cervical ectopic pregnancy that could have killed her.

On the morning of the twelfth day she was in the hospital, before I could even send Nora a message to make sure she was awake and ready for me to come over, she had sent me one.

They released me this morning. Are you home?

With a lifetime of long nights under my belt, those eleven that Nora was in the hospital might have been the longest. I don't know what they would have been like if I wasn't sober. I retained everything the doctors said because I didn't have cobwebs from bong hits. I was there for someone I loved in ways I knew I never could have been if I were drunk or high. Nora was the person I always wanted to be with, so I needed to be the person I always thought I could be.

• • •

I was over two months off weed, over a month off caffeine, and nine days off biting my nails. I was picking change up off the ground like nobody's business. Scratching my back felt so good it could have been considered a religious experience. I didn't have to hide my fingers from people. I felt like in a couple months I would be ready for the cover of *Nails Weekly*, the magazine by and for people with immaculate nails.

I was watching fellow admitted nail-biter LeBron James try to knock off a juggernaut Warriors team in game four of the NBA finals when it happened again. I heard Nora say from behind the bathroom door, "I'm bleeding a lot and it really hurts."

There weren't as many laughs this time around.

We said "I love you" for the first time that night in the emergency room. I said it for a lot of reasons. The best reason was because I felt it, and I was pretty sure she did, too. The worst reason was because I was now scared this could be my only chance.

After we'd spent two weeks in ambulances, emergency rooms, and a shared hospital room, it felt like we were on *Extreme Makeover: Home Edition* when we got our own private room at six a.m. You can tell how tough a situation is by what you consider to be good news. I was in a "Great! There's a chair I can sleep on" tough situation. Nora was in an "At least this drug addict who knocked me up told me he loves me" tough situation. I know, and that chair barely even reclined.

Another team of doctors whose relationships with each other were crushingly platonic came in to give us their latest empty prognosis. Every day that Nora's hCG didn't go down was more dangerous than the last, and the chemo still wasn't working.

That night, Nora wanted me to go home, even though we had our own room.

"You need to sleep in your bed," she said.

"I want to sleep here."

"I want you to sleep at home."

I walked home from the hospital. My bending will was broken.

This is my fault. I should have let this woman live her life. I'm cursed and I curse everyone I love. She's going to die and it's my fault. These fucking doctors. They told us she was all better. Just like they said my uncle was all better. I can't spend tonight alone in my room, wondering if this fucking asshole god is going to take another person I love away from me.

Tears began to fall down my face, and I lowered my head. I had made it to my destination: the bar.

Play the tape out. I don't wanna play the fucking tape out. *Play the tape out.* I'm sick of playing the tape out. *Play the tape out.* Fine, I'll play the tape out.

It was the quickest, and the most horrifying, of all the times I'd ever done it: I get drunk and Nora calls me crying, asking me to come back to the hospital, but I'm too drunk, and I leave her alone and scared.

Within an hour of playing that scenario out in my mind, it played out in real life. Nora called me and asked me to come back to the hospital. I didn't even finish my drink; I just raced there. What did I care? There would be other peppermint teas in my life.

The next morning I woke up on the wrong side of the chair but tried to remain in good spirits. That was the day the article about my podcast came out in the *Toronto Star*. I bought a newspaper from the stand in the hospital and brought it upstairs. Nora thought it was great, but I thought I sounded stupid and looked ugly. But I was happy she was happy. I was surprised by what the writer hadn't included from our interview.

She'd asked me, "What scares you the most about quitting all of this stuff?"

"That I'll finally be sober, I'll have my life together, I'll be in love, and my career will take off. It still won't be enough and I'll relapse."

Maybe it was too dark.

● ● ●

The next morning we were woken up by doctors coming in to tell us about the latest round of "Look, this probably won't be necessary, but." This time, the number one vaginal surgeon in the country (look, I'd love to slide in an immature joke here, but it's not the time) and another specialized doctor told us the hCG count just wasn't getting to where it needed to be.

"What is the worst-case scenario?" Nora asked.

"We don't like to deal in hypothetical worst-case situations," the doctor said.

"I know that, but everything that has happened to me so far has been worst-case scenario. What is the worst-case scenario?" she asked again.

The doctors confirmed that the worst-case scenario was a full hysterectomy. That information took all the air out of the room.

"If worst comes to worst, you don't have to—" Nora tried to tell me before I interrupted.

"Don't. I don't care if you get a full hysterectomy, or if they have to remove ninety-five percent of your body and you're just a loose-leaf head. I love you. I'm not going anywhere," I said, before we both raced to make the same floating head blow-job joke.

The following morning the numbers hadn't moved enough. It was the same thing the day after. On the fifth day of the second hospital stay we officially got the news. Even though we were prepared for anything, it was still stunning to hear it out loud. It was always a possibility—in fact, it was always the most likely outcome. But it was still a shock when a nurse came in and told us:

"You can go home now."

Overnight, Nora's hCG numbers had plummeted and were still falling fast. She was going to have a long road to physical and emotional recovery, but Nora was still so excited to leave, she did so with the IV lock still in her arm.

I had been counting the days a lot lately. Finally making it 730 days off cocaine was a notable one, for sure. Thirty days off booze feels good when it's the longest you've ever gone. But what felt the best was waking up beside Nora in bed, one day after she'd been in the hospital.

chapter 11

cigarettes

Of all the things I thought I would never be that I ended up being, cigarette smoker was the hardest to take. Growing up I wanted to be a non-smoker as much as I wanted to be a Stanley Cup champion goaltender, but the only rings on my fingers were nicotine stains. Some of my lowest moments of addiction have come from cigarettes: I've smoked cigarette butts off the street—a few times I wasn't even drunk. All right, district attorney, it was a lot of times! When I would do hard drugs I would chain-smoke upwards of forty cigarettes in one night. Even at my worst, I never pictured myself in my golden years in a retirement home somewhere, all coked up while speed-talking about Batman as an allegory for the French Revolution. Cigarettes, though? Those were going with me to the grave (or I was going with them). The way I used to see it, I might never *want* to quit alcohol or weed, but I would never be *able* to quit cigarettes.

After dalliances with cigarettes in my teens I became a heavy smoker at the age of twenty-one. I had been putting tobacco in my joints for years before this, but that was when I started prioritizing cigarettes above health, food, finances, personal odour, and focus. Anytime difficulty arose, I thought cigarettes had the answer. I would tell cigarettes all my problems, and they would always come back with the same advice: *Have another smoke. Let's figure this thing out.* When I worked at the call centre my lunch break was four cigarettes in a row.

When I was seventeen I got on a plane for the first time. It was a tiny propeller plane flown by an airline that runs to small towns in Northern Ontario and was named after an animal that is famous for not flying. As the plane took off it sounded more like an old lawn mower running over a Rollerblade than what the Wright brothers probably had in mind, but I was excited to be flying for the first time. I loved looking out the window and down at the clouds that were somehow beneath us. I had been in cars that were bigger than this plane that was suddenly caught in an electrical storm. There was extreme turbulence and we had to circle the Ottawa airport for a long time as we waited for the storm to pass before we could land. But I didn't flinch once; I even thought it was kind of fun.

The next time I flew was for shows in my early twenties and I had two severe panic attacks. On one flight I got up and speed-walked to the bathroom while the seat belt sign was on as a flight attendant protested. I was about to light a cigarette in the bathroom and just deal with Guantanamo Bay as long as I could bring my smokes. Reason prevailed when I told myself, *You can have all the smokes you want when we land.* Calm washed over me. I returned to my seat and apologized to the crew.

As I chain-smoked at the airport I wondered why I had become such a bad flyer considering how much I'd loved it the first time. Despite my enormous powers of denial, I was able to connect the obvious dots: clearly, I needed to hear the propeller to feel comfortable flying. Sadly, it took me years to see that what I thought was a fear of flying was actually a fear of being trapped without cigarettes. That's how massive their hold was on me: my brain equated the feelings of not smoking with the feelings of dying.

When you're trying to quit something, it can be hard to focus on "one day at a time." You know it's what you're supposed to do, but if you always did what you're supposed to do, you wouldn't be a smoker. You need more logic than just the basics of one day at a time. I thought about what a burden being a smoker for the rest of my life would be versus how hard it would be to quit. All the ex-smokers I had spoken to told me the same thing: after a couple of years they didn't even think about smoking anymore, and if they did, it actually seemed repulsive to them, the same way it does to non-smokers. They truly didn't even want to anymore. My reasoning, then, was this: quitting smoking would be a plea bargain. I could have two years fighting decreasingly difficult cravings or a life sentence of being a smoker. I would plead it down.

The first three days off cigarettes are the toughest physically— but not tougher than the recovery after a cervical ectopic pregnancy and chemo. Nora was bedridden and relapsing after being in the hospital; she had turned back to the kratom. So on July 1, we had a quitting party. I was quitting cigarettes, and Nora was quitting kratom. We didn't have a lot of dinner parties with other couples planned for a bit.

The withdrawal from cigarettes is different than that of booze or hard drugs. DTs and the other worst physical withdrawal symptoms of alcohol come in waves. Nicotine withdrawal, though not as intense, is more constant. The irritability alone can be enough to make anyone crack by sundown on the first day. The first few days played out the way they usually did when I was trying to quit something difficult. I was supplementing cigarettes with nicotine gum, ice cream, and anger. I wasn't scared of this part, though—I knew this wasn't the toughest test. No, the toughest part for me was always nights like the one six days later when my penis and testicles were tightly locked in a male chastity belt. This is not a metaphor.

Theme shows are all the rage in comedy these days. It turns out that in an over-saturated comedy market people are getting tired of the stale formula of a person onstage all alone saying funny things. Now, every new show in comedy has a hook. There's a convoluted premise, like all the comedians play the ukulele while they perform and the show has a name like *Fourth Stringers* that makes you want to karate chop yourself in the neck. On day nine off cigarettes I agreed to do one of these shows. The premise of this one was that my friend Jarrett and I would wear chastity belts while being read dating horror stories and critique the man's etiquette on the date. Afterwards, a panel of female comedians would vote on which one of us got the key to unlock their belt first.

"Snug" can be a word with many interpretations. If I were to say, "I was so snug in bed last night," it might conjure an image of me with my eyes closed, mouth smiling widely, nestled into my warm bed with the covers pulled tightly up to my neck. Now, if I were to say, "My penis and testicles fit too snugly into the chastity belt," it would conjure a less wholesome sight. The show came and went. I wasn't funny and the crowd didn't like me. It was made all the worse by the pain that was flowing through my nether regions.

After the show I was swelling but not with pride. My right testicle was in blinding pain, and I was angry at my performance, the crowd, the entire world. That was the confluence of feelings that led me to wanting a cigarette the very most, in days prior. I was close to giving in that night, so I played the tape out. Something different happened this time.

I'm on my fourth smoke in a row. I'm angry that the cigarettes haven't actually made anything better, but I'm still convinced lighting the fifth will do it. Nope, not that one either. My lungs hurt and the following day I can't even go to the gym. On days I know I'm not going to the gym I have a cigarette as soon as I wake up. When I have one as soon as I wake up I'm a goner for the day, just chasing that dragon dressed as a camel. The next day plays out the same way. I can clearly see how shitty my next two weeks will be, stemming from lighting this one cigarette. But that's why I'll have just this one. I'm stressed right now, so stressed that I need a cigarette. I don't want it; I need it.

Wait—how did you get in here?

It was the first time that, as I played the tape out, the addict voice found his way inside. Previously, I had hidden the office where I play the tape out in my brain so the addict couldn't find it. But I guess after eighteen months of searching he finally came bursting through the door in his ill-fitting, grease-stained grey suit and crooked tie.

"I looked everywhere for you! First I went to the pleasure centre 'cause you're always there, but I asked Booze where you were and he said he hasn't seen you in a while. I checked painful memories before I ended up here in res ... resp ... I can't pronounce this word."

"Responsibility," I said, rolling my eyes.

"Yeah, that thing. Is this a new building or something?"

"It's been here a while, actually. It was just vacant."

"Crazy. Never even been to this part of town. Anyway, I got some cigarettes with me. Let's smoke."

I want cigarettes all the time, but I don't want to want them all the time. Having a cigarette won't change either of those things; in fact, it will only make them worse. I reminded myself that two years in jail is way better than a lifetime. I played out an image of me resisting this craving, and the next one, and the next one, until I'm a couple years down the line. In my mind's eye, I get to a place where I next-to-never even think about having a smoke and it's not hard anymore.

The addict voice storms out of the office. "Fine. I'm going to see what the penis and balls are up to. Hey fellas, how are—oh my God, you look terrible. Is that a chastity belt?"

• • •

There are few times in life when you're in a room full of people and every single person is thinking the exact same thing. That hot day in the middle of July I knew every one of us had the same thought screaming in our brains in unison:

Don't do it! There's gotta be a better answer than this.

It felt like it was happening in slow motion and we all had to sit there, frozen, just watching in horror.

Her lips slowly parted and she said the words her friends and family hoped for her sake she wouldn't.

"I do."

With that, Alexis agreed to marry Dylan.

The wedding was as beautiful as an event could be that was attended by a man with *Dylicious*, actually, in real life, tattooed on his lower back. It was elegantly smart like Alexis, and there were doughnuts there like Dylan. Other than the sheer terror I felt on behalf of my friend Alexis, it was a sensational night. Nora and I danced for hours in a manner that was sexually inappropriate for a wedding. And I laughed with one of my oldest, dumbest, baldest but always-there-for-me friends on his big day. You just know I have to bring up that it was my first sober wedding.

Smartphones have led to me finding out about a number of significant life events while sitting on the toilet. It happened again the morning after the wedding, but this time it was good news. I got the phone call I had been waiting eight years for: I was invited back to perform at Just for Laughs, and this time I would be taping for Kevin Hart's LOL Network.

Marito had crashed on my couch the night before. The festival had already invited him a few weeks earlier. After everything we'd been through over the past couple of years, it felt right that we'd be going together. I thought of the best way I could tell him.

"How are you getting to Montreal next week?" I asked him.

"They booked me a train ticket."

"Oh, okay, I'll see if they can book me on the same train."

"Bro, they only book people that are booked for the fest."

"I know," I said smiling.

Marito just stared at me, confused. So I smiled harder and opened my eyes wider and nodded my head.

"Yoooooooooooooooo," Marito said before hug-tackling me.

After the initial rush had given way to relief, the doubts crept in. This was the biggest show of my life, and it was in ten days. Could I do it without cigarettes? I was only two weeks into performing without them, and I still wasn't entirely comfortable without them as part of my pre-show routine. What happens after I kill the biggest show of my life? No booze, no weed, no smokes, no nothing? No way. I'm bringing one cigar to enjoy after my show at the hotel party.

Dom was another old friend of mine who was booked for the festival, and he came on the podcast before we left for Montreal. Dom and I had fallen out over the last five years: disagreements had turned into fights, which turned into hurtful comments, which turned into a broken friendship, which turned into a non-existent relationship. We were both angry guys who eventually turned our guns on each other.

But Dom had reached out to me when my podcast first came out. I knew he had been through a lot over the past two years, and he'd had to say goodbye to people before he was ready. Cancer gets around, it seems. Dom's abusive mom died five days before we recorded the episode about him quitting his anger. The episode was everything Dom is: inappropriate, hilarious, and raw. And it ended on a personal note when Dom said, "When you texted me that one time 'You were never there for me'—I'm really sorry I wasn't there for you, Alex. I kind of wasn't there for me either."

"I wasn't there for me either" was instantly tattooed on my brain. I knew I hadn't always been there for myself. How can you be there for the people you love if you don't even do it for yourself? I still wasn't sure if I was really there for myself, but I was glad Dom was.

A week later, Nora and I—and the biggest comedians in the world—arrived in Montreal for the Just for Laughs festival. I was a raging addict and alcoholic last time I was there, so I didn't know there was a whole festival happening outside the bars. The streets were flooded with performers of all kinds, and there were fair games and even a mini roller coaster that Nora and I went on three times in a row because we shared a certain personality trait. My warm-up show before the taping was later that night. I went after a well-known, fast-emerging comic whose Netflix special was blowing up. But there wasn't even a sliver of daylight between his set and mine. Or between those of the SNL cast members who went on later in the show. I was holding my own with some real heavyweights.

"Y'all ain't got no love for Death Row? Y'all ain't got no love for Dr. Dre and Snoop Dogg?" is what I said the following afternoon for my sound check, to a big laugh from the crew. The show was eight hours away, but I was already dialed in. I went back to my hotel and took my pre-show nap as soon as my head hit the pillow. I woke up, showered, put on the outfit I'd carefully picked out, and walked to the show with the swagger in my step breaking only when I had to tiptoe around a puddle to keep my brand-new shoes sparkling white.

I entered the beautiful Théâtre Berri and went backstage for makeup. Then I nailed my interview that would also air on the network. I was loose and funny, feeling it, in the pocket. Nothing was going to stop me from having the set of the festival. Every talent scout, agent, and comedian in North America was going to charge at each other wielding various weapons in a battle out of The Lord of the Rings to work with me after I was done.

"He could be the leading man. Or the best friend. I want him," the woman from the movie business says as she maces a man in the face.

"Has anyone asked this guy if he can sing? He looks like he's got a voice that we in the biz call a panty dropper," the lady from the recording industry exclaims before impaling a horse with a harpoon and beating the armoured knight that falls from it with her bare hands.

"What's the deal with how badly I want this guy to be the new Kramer in a *Seinfeld* reboot?" Jerry Seinfeld says before ripping a man's still-beating heart out of his chest.

Backstage I was making the makeup artists laugh as they powdered my face. There was a buzz in the air, equal parts excitement and nerves. Kevin Hart strolled through with his entourage to check out the stage and make sure everything was running smoothly, and with that blessing, the show began. I was in the green room, watching as each comedian came back after their set and it was easy to see the reaction they'd gotten from the crowd by their faces. My set was late in the show, and this crowd was losing steam with every "Is everyone here on Tinder?" It didn't faze me, though, as I'd lived this very moment of redemption in my head every single day for the last eight years. This was the culmination of my battle with substance abuse. I was the prodigious, prodigal, fallen addict who wouldn't let the curtain close before the second act he had up his sleeve.

I was on next. I was standing beside the floor director, and the fact that the crowd was dead didn't have me questioning my confidence for even a second. The talent shows in school, the thousands of miles I'd travelled across the frozen hellscape that is the Canadian winter, the countless talks with Jocko, the drugs, the booze, the breakups, the dropouts, the relapses, and the times I almost gave up—they had all brought me to this moment.

The last thing I saw before I went onstage was Nora's face, and it was everything I needed. I walked out, grabbed the mic clean out of the stand—and had a completely mediocre set.

I was in the alley afterwards, smoking the cigar I'd brought. Commiseration cigars taste much worse than celebration ones, especially when you inhale them deeply because you want to feel the pain. I was coughing as I rehearsed my showbiz bullshit "Great! Oh, it was so much fun," answer for when people asked me how my set was.

I considered this to be one of the greatest failings of my life, but I had to hide that under gritted teeth forced into the best smile I could muster. I had told anyone who would listen that if Just for Laughs gave me one more chance, I would have the set of the festival. I was a fucking fraud. What a difference twenty minutes can make. The only reason I didn't have a cigarette in that alley was because I knew that if I did, a drink wouldn't be far behind. I had to pull out the emergency logic. I promised myself if I still felt like this in the morning, I would drink or use or both.

Nora tried to tell me that my set was great, but I knew she was just trying to make me feel better. I didn't bomb, or even struggle.

I did good, considering how dead that crowd was, deep into a long show—really good. But really good wasn't good enough. David Letterman didn't get called over to Johnny Carson's desk because he was really good. I needed to be great, and I wasn't. For that set there was no difference for me between really good and total failure. That night I stared at my hotel room ceiling for hours, wondering how I could have missed the biggest shot of my life.

I was funny on my radio appearance two days later, but it was too little, too late. No one gets discovered at the festival because they nailed their radio interview. Even being named one of the "Canadians to Watch" at the festival by a comedy publication didn't make me feel like less of a failure. So I turned to heart-attack casserole—or, as Canadians call, it poutine. As always, filling my belly with deep-fried food eased the pain. Emotionally speaking, of course. Physically, I was on the toilet screaming to the sky, "Father, why have you forsaken me?" and then I was left with the same feeling as before, plus the agony in my stomach.

Later that night, I was walking through the outdoor carnival part of the festival. It had looked different a couple days ago during the daytime, crowded with people and illuminated with sunshine. Now it looked like a ghost town, until I saw a familiar face with an unfamiliar look on his face.

"I just don't know if this feeling is ever going to go away," Marito said, tears welling in his eyes.

I'd seen Marito's set earlier in the night. Much like my set two nights ago, his was really good. Much like me, he felt that wasn't good enough.

"It's not even about the show, man," Marito said. "If the show went amazing and I won, I'd still feel like this. I'm fucking here. I did it. Why does it feel empty?"

I didn't have an answer for Marito, or for myself. We reaffirmed the things we'd heard in AA and said to each other so many times, but in a hollow tone. I told him I'd meet up with him in an hour, and I made him promise to call me if he felt like he was going to slip.

The second-to-last night of Just for Laughs is the biggest party of the festival. But I had a podcast to record first. Bobby is from a planet that can't possibly be in our galaxy. A maniacal genius in the best way, onstage and off. We'd done drugs together and bonded over the craziness of our childhoods. He had the most original voice of any comedian I knew. Bobby's career was a five-alarm fire by this point. How could it not be? Everyone saw Bobby's success coming from miles away, but it didn't make it any less exciting to watch. When he would come to Ottawa, we would do magic mushrooms and sleep at my mom's house, and now he was on all of the UK's biggest panel shows, had taped for so many things in so many places, and he had his own show coming out on Comedy Central UK. He was newly married, sober for two and a half years, and doing the best work of his career.

For all of these reasons and more, there was no one I would have rather recorded an episode with at Just for Laughs.

During the interview, Bobby said something I will keep with me for the rest of my life.

"I always have this thing, where I'm always being like, 'Oh it's so hard.' It's not that anything's actually that hard. It's that I convinced myself everything's really hard so I can get fucked up. I'm telling myself this story of 'I'm such a victim, life's really hard. It's so hard. In fact, I need this. I need whatever I'm doing. I need a big fat line of coke. I need to get hammered. I need to go fucking have a one-night stand and cheat on some lady I've been dating. I need that,' you know? But, really, life's pretty good. I'm just telling myself this victim story so that I can eventually get to the point where I say 'fuck it.' This week's been pretty great. I might not have felt great, but that's because of the story I'm telling myself. The reality of it is, you know, I'm at a festival with all my best friends, getting paid to do the thing I love."

I didn't even know this was what I had been doing for so long until I heard Bobby say it. In that moment, I understood this was what I had been doing that entire week at Just for Laughs. Was I really ready to risk my life by relapsing all because the jokes I told didn't get the kind of laughs I wanted? Of course I wasn't. That sneaky addict voice takes many forms, and this was the first time I realized that piece of shit will intentionally make me feel worse if it means it gets to use.

I told Bobby about how much I'd been beating myself up this week, and he related but also told me how his perspective on comedy had changed.

"I think the mistake I make when I feel that way is that I'm thinking that my job is in some way supposed to change who I am. I'm thinking, 'Oh man, my career has gotten to this point. That means I'm a better person. That means I'm better. That means I'm good.' It's just a job. It doesn't matter. It's not who I am. It's just something I do. Who I am is like how I am with my family and my friends. That's what's important."

By this time I had received emails from listeners to the podcast from every continent not covered in ice. The stories had become more personal and the gratitude deeper. A couple of people even told me that my podcast was like what "Party in the USA" had been to me. And here I was, ready to relapse because my stand-up comedy set didn't go exactly the way I wanted it to? The stand-up comedy set that I was performing at the biggest comedy festival in the world like I'd always dreamed? One year after my uncle died.

What my dad had been trying to tell me for years finally sunk in: person first, comedian second.

I left Bobby's hotel room and went to the after-party. The first person I saw was Marito. He told me he was good, and I could tell because of the dancing. I heard he murdered his taping the next night.

The next person I saw was Nora, and she had saved me a couple of tacos. "Get those in you before you quit red meat," she said.

It was the first party of the week where I didn't even think about drugs and alcohol. I danced with my best friends and the woman I loved at the biggest comedy festival in the world. The talent shows in school, the thousands of miles I'd travelled across the frozen hellscape that is the Canadian winter, the countless talks with Jocko, the drugs, the booze, the breakups, the dropouts, the relapses, and the times I almost gave up—I was wrong when I thought a seven-minute stand-up set was the culmination of all those moments.

Just like I'd be wrong to think there was any culmination to all those moments. Sure, they shaped who I am as much as anything else, but that's all they were, just moments. There wouldn't be a comedy show, a craving conquered, a song on the radio, or some quote from a boxer that would be able to magically reach into my past and my future to forever change me into a perfect person who was done hurting or growing. There was never going to be something that came along, good or bad, that made me some kind of final version of myself.

It took me day 892 off cocaine, day 582 off booze, day 115 off weed, day 85 off caffeine, day 55 off nail biting, and day 25 off cigarettes to truly understand the meaning of one day at a time.

Today is the only day I can live, and this today is a damn good one.

● ● ●

I'd never gotten to this stage of quitting smoking before, where the cravings stopped happening every day. Maybe one thing that helped was that this time I had someone quit smoking with me, and it was the person I'd always wished would. After forty years as a heavy smoker, my mom was my guest for episode eighteen of my podcast.

The interview was funny and heartwarming. Until the ending, which quickly turned into threats of mutually assured destruction.

"I will start smoking two packs a day. If you go back on drinking or smoking," my mom said.

"Well, I'll start doing cocaine again. I'll shoot fucking heroin in my goddamn eyeball if you even have a cigarette," I said.

"Honest to God, I will take you out."

A beautiful promise between a mother and son devolved into a homicide pact in less than thirty seconds. But the interview ended on a more sentimental note when I told my mom why I wanted her to quit smoking all along.

"I need you around for as long as possible, because no one gets me like you do," I said.

It was the last time we'd ever speak.

On the podcast, I mean. Relax, only one more person dies in this book.

But first, I will try to tell you about beating meat without resorting to another immature joke. If I can quit smoking cigarettes, I can resist that temptation, too.

chapter 12

red meat

I barely talked about red meat on my podcast because, to be honest, I never considered eating red meat to be something that I was out of control with, necessarily. It wasn't the health implications either. There's evidence to show a causal link between red meat and certain cancers and heart disease, but the main reason it was on my quit list was different from all the others. I wanted to keep the scope of my project to addiction and personal health, so I didn't bring it up, but according to the UN, "Red meat requires 28 times more land to produce than pork or chicken, 11 times more water and results in five times more climate-warming emissions."

I never gave much of a fuck about plastic straws and the large carbon footprint a hamburger leaves. I'm just trying to keep up with that honesty policy here. Every year, 4.5 trillion cigarettes butts are littered, with a lot of those ending up in our oceans, leaking toxic chemicals into the water. In any given year I could have been responsible for a few million of those. The worst part was I recognized that climate change was an existential threat to humans. I just didn't think humans could stop being humans, so why should I? I can try some mental gymnastics and make my justifications, but let's just call me what I really was. Part of the problem. I didn't want to be part of the problem anymore. Which makes telling you about the airplane I took next a tad awkward.

The flight to New York was bumpy and I unconsciously bit my nails a few times. Whenever Nora told me I was doing it, I couldn't believe it. How did I not know? Every six inches the plane dropped sent me spiralling. I hadn't been scared on a flight in years—what was happening? I realized that I may have picked an inopportune time to quit nicotine gum. But the nicotine-withdrawal flight was a worthy trade-off for my destination: Nora and I were going to stay with her uncle in the Hamptons for a weekend before going down to New York City.

There are few things in life that live up to their hype, but for my money, the ocean would be at the top of the list.

I love the water. I was always the last kid in the pool the lifeguard had to tell for the fifth time to get out because the public swim was over. Go figure. I had seen the Atlantic many times on my tours of the East Coast but never gotten to go in it. I swam out the farthest out of anyone in the water, and I was warned to watch out for the undertow because it could get even the best of swimmers. That might be true, but I'm sure those swimmers never got their green badge like I did. I don't even remember what level green was, but it must have signified something important if it required a badge. The sheer vastness and majesty of the ocean made me feel insignificant, but every wave that touched down on me made me feel lucky to be alive.

I got to experience that because I got sober. And because I met the next guest on my podcast: Nora.

Of all the amazing recoveries I had seen that gave me inspiration, Nora's stood out. She was on day thirty-seven off kratom and day two off cigarettes. Nora was only twenty-three days off chemo when she decided to get off kratom. She had lost one of her best friends to an overdose less than a year before, had a cervical ectopic pregnancy, was forced into an opioid relapse because of it, and was still fighting PTSD from the whole thing. And in eight months.

Something Nora said towards the end of the podcast stuck out to me the most.

"You come into this world and leave this world alone, and you can have support all throughout, but you have to fucking woman or man up and do the shit yourself. And that is actually how you quit something. It gives you a sense of fear but also a sense of control. Like you're the only person who can take the reins on this thing. You know, shit's going to come your way, but you have control over how you react to it. That's it. That's all you have is control over the way you deal with shit."

If you're a prizefighter, you have an entire team of people to support you 24/7. You have a driver, a cook, a bodyguard, a promoter, an old Southern guy who yells barely comprehensible motivational lines, friends, family, and most importantly, your trainer. They believe in you, they support you, they intentionally lose to you in any game of chance or skill to keep your self-esteem at its highest. And they love you. They even walk you to the squared circle. But then you hear the bell and you walk across the ring to your opponent to start the fight. It's the worst part about the sport because you're putting your life on the line when you start that walk. Scariest of all, you make that walk alone.

There are going to be times when your go-to person who talks you out of relapsing doesn't answer their phone. And then your backup person doesn't, either. It's one a.m., you can't sleep, you're three months sober, the pink cloud has just worn off, and you're starting to resent this whole sobriety bullshit. You've just had the worst day and the bar or the dealer seems like a good option for the first time in a while. It's going to be a long night staring up at the ceiling trying to want to not want. You make that walk alone, too.

Three days later, Nora and I ripped a storytelling show in Queens with Jhanelle before we went down to that spot by the water with the breath-stealing view of the city. I'd stood in this same spot only three months before, when I was forty days sober, staring out at the millions of lights and lives, still with that longing to get fucked up because the moment felt like it was missing something. I'd done what I always did and thought that something missing meant it had to be replaced with drugs or booze.

This time, staring out at New York City with Nora at my side, nothing was missing.

I'm an addict, though, which means I always want more. So just like the last time I left the city, I knew I wanted to get back there again.

chapter 13

dairy

It took me a long time to know how to start this chapter, for a few reasons. People had voiced such confusion over dairy being included on my list of things to quit. I can't say for sure that I was ever physically addicted to dairy, but it feels just as weird trying to pretend I didn't have a problem with it.

Let's take a look at the World Health Organization's Alcohol Use Disorders Identification Test that's used to screen for unhealthy alcohol use but replace alcohol with dairy.

1. How often do you eat food with dairy?

(0)   Never

(1)   Monthly or less

(2)   Two to four times a month

(3)   Two to three times a week

(4)   Four times a week or more ✓

Yeah, but to be fair, most people probably check that box.

2. On days you do eat dairy, how much?

(1)   One meal

(2)   Two meals ✓

(3)   Three meals

(4)   More than three meals

Ha! Joke's on you. I never eat three meals in a day 'cause then I can't get drunk. I'm doing great here.

3. How often do you consume more dairy than is needed to be full?

(0)   Never

(2)   Monthly

(3)   Weekly

(4)   Daily ✓

I guess that depends on your definition of "full," but yeah, I eat until it hurts, so I guess that counts.

4. How often in the last year did you find you couldn't stop consuming dairy after you started?

(0)   Never

(2)   Monthly

(3)   Weekly

(4)   Daily ✓

Does the ice cream being all gone count as stopping?

5. How often in the last year did you find yourself unable to do what was expected of you because of dairy?

(0)   Never

(2)   Monthly

(3)   Weekly ✓

(4)   Daily

All right, fine, I tend to be late for things because I'm on the toilet in pain.

6. How often do you need to start your day with dairy?

(0)   Never

(2)   Monthly

(3)   Weekly ✓

(4)   Daily

Again, two meals a day means no breakfast. That's two in a row without checking "Daily," so suck on that!

7. How often in the last year did you feel remorse after eating dairy?

(0)   Never

(2)   Monthly

(3)   Weekly

(4)   Daily ✓

Ah, fuck.

8. How many times in the last year were you not able to remember the night before because of dairy?

(0)   Never ✓

(2)   Monthly

(3)   Weekly

(4)   Daily

All right, maybe not changing this question was cheating, but check a "Never" off for this guy.

9. Have you injured yourself from eating dairy?

(0)   No

(4)   Yes ✓

Ulcers and high blood pressure barely count as injuries, though.

10. Has a doctor ever been concerned about your eating dairy and suggested you cut down?

(0)   No

(4)   Yes ✓

Pfft, doctors. What do they know?

A score of twenty or more qualifies as dependence. I scored thirty-two, and that would have been higher if pizza caused memory loss. I've used unhealthy food for comfort, for celebration, and as a numbing agent in my life. Overeating is in my blood the same way as chemical dependence. I quit dairy for a while, and just like drugs, smokes, and alcohol, it was hard but easier than I thought it would be. I started to change my relationship to food and tried to see it as fuel for my body instead of pleasure for my mind.

Because that's all food ever was to me—another source of pleasure. I made all the same mistakes with food as I did with drugs. The ten minutes or less it took me to finish a fast food order for two during which my brain's pleasure receptors would be firing astronomically was worth the rush of depression and self-loathing I dealt with after. And the hours of pain on the toilet. And the health implications. And the money problems. And the low self-esteem. Then I'm sad. I hate this feeling so much I would do anything to get away from it. And I'm on the phone ordering pizza.

To close out August, I had the unhealthiest two-week stretch of eating in longer than I could remember. Ice cream, pizza, candy, chips, poutine, pancakes—and I'm just talking about one day. The only time I wasn't miserable was when I had something deliciously awful in my mouth. At least I wasn't eating red meat, which meant I was personally producing less pollution. It wasn't a significant amount, but I know better than anyone that you have to inch your way to results. But my room was messier, I wasn't going to the gym or doing shows as often, and I had gained weight. I ate myself into a minor depression. Without booze or drugs around to blame for why I felt so empty inside, it became clear to me just how much I abused food.

Were those first few days in September off dairy as difficult as my first few days off hard drugs or booze? No. But there's a flip side to that coin. Anytime the addict inside of me said, "I need" about drugs or alcohol, I could tell that voice, "No, you don't actually need it." I did some research for this book, and it turns out you do actually need to eat. In that respect it's more challenging to get off shitty food.

Still, kicking dairy wasn't going to be the hardest part about September. Being without Nora was. I was booked on a tour of Western Canada for the first time in my career, and it was going to be five straight weekends headlining, the longest and farthest I'd ever been away from home. I was excited to not try Alberta beef or BC weed. The flight out there was easy because I had nicotine gum and a toothpick.

Oh right, I haven't told you about the toothpicks yet. Being hyperaware of my thoughts and feeling in the first few days off smokes, I saw how much of it was an oral fixation. I bought so much gum and sugary treats they rephrased the cliché to be "like an Alex Wood in a candy store." I knew I was making the same mistakes I always had with quitting cigarettes—simply replacing them with something unhealthy for two weeks before I cracked and went back to my rat poison–laced master.

After breakfast one day, out of total desperation, I put a toothpick in my mouth. Nothing happened. *I might as well take this stupid twig out of my mouth,* I thought. But I could feel the same neurons that fire pleasure from a cigarette go off when I took the toothpick out of my mouth, and then put it back in. I had done this motion hundreds of thousands of times with a cigarette and it led to immeasurable pleasure. Pavlov was just ringing that same bell in my brain because the toothpick stopped my craving in its tracks. I couldn't believe how stupid the addict inside of me was.

I'd been letting this moron be the boss of me for years? It was like every time I wanted a smoke it was five p.m. on Friday and my hard-ass boss came in screaming, "What have you been working on all week?"

And then I handed him a used condom.

"Whoa, this is good stuff. I'm going to send this up the ladder to corporate."

The only problem with having a toothpick in my mouth in public was people thinking I was about to spontaneously break into a number from *West Side Story*.

When the plane landed in Calgary it had been the best flight of my life. Better celebrate what a great flyer I am with a cigar, which I'd justified smoking a lot for the past month since my friend Ryan's wedding. Oh, twenty dollars for a pack of eight? No, thank you. It was the cold splash of water to my face that I needed to get off cigars.

I was staying with one of my oldest friends from high school. Now, Grant might be the best guy I know, but he's still a friend of mine. For example, his daughter couldn't pronounce her *l*'s yet. Grant demonstrated this with great glee by having his daughter talk about her favourite character from *Beauty and the Beast*. The clock. You can do the mental math on why Grant and I thought this was so hilarious and what is wrong with us for it.

The shows in Calgary were as well attended as they could be while Garth Brooks was in town. They must really like them some

Garth Brooks in Calgary because, I swear to God, that guy was running seventeen shows a day.

The comedy club manager told me, "Yeah, the late show tonight is going to be a little bit light 'cause people are resting up for Garth's brunch show tomorrow."

But two people told me they came to the club because they were fans of my podcast, and that it was the first time they went out to a place that served alcohol since they got sober. They said if I could do it, they could do it.

It reminded me of the ripple effect that sobriety can have and the wondrous symbiotic relationship between addicts. Have you ever seen the movie *The Human Centipede*? It's like that. We're all attached to this human centipede, only instead of somebody eating something and then shitting into somebody else's mouth, they're shitting out inspiration and good vibes. If that image was too gross, we're going to Lake Louise next, so calm down.

Lake Louise could be a screen saver on God's laptop it's that gorgeous. The sprawling and massive snow-covered Rocky Mountains surround a lake that looks like it belongs in Bermuda because the water is a sparkling combination of powder blue and aqua green. It's a good thing there were stunning vistas to behold because I was about to do an eight-kilometre hike to the peak of Devil's Thumb.

Devil's Thumb may sound like a sex act that requires antibacterial hand soap afterwards (another thing I wrote before every act, sexual or not, required antibacterial hand soap), but it's one of the most challenging ascents at Lake Louise. It didn't take me long to start feeling the altitude. Every time I tried to draw a deep breath, it felt like I was breathing through a narrow straw in one nostril. Panic started to set in. The only thing that kept me going was remembering how many times over the past two years I'd thought I couldn't do something, and then did it. How many times I'd felt uncomfortable, scared, or that I couldn't keep going. That and there were several young children running up the trail quite easily.

My body acclimated to the altitude as Grant and I laughed about dumb things from the old days. We came to the end of the hike and the view was all right, but to be honest, I'd thought it would be better.

"Oh no, now we go up there," Grant said, pointing at an eighty-degree climb.

"I can't make it."

I was wearing sneakers that I'd inherited from my brother seventeen years before and had no traction. Everyone else I saw was wearing hiking boots. Although I was four days off cigars, there was still smoke floating in my lungs, telling all my organs how he could make them a big star. Beads of sweat were collecting on my forehead. I tried once more to gain better footing and simply kicked more mud and rocks down the almost-vertical incline. I was holding onto a branch that was sticking out of the ground, and it was the only thing stopping me from taking a dangerous human toboggan trip down the mountain.

To my left, I could see a bit of a trail that led back down. If I slowly eased my way there, I could go to the bottom and wait for Grant.

Fuck it. I lunged upwards with all my strength, clawing with my fingernails and trying to dig the tip of my shoes as far into the ground as possible. I repeated this move three more times until I reached a small shelf where I rested. Finally, I scaled the jagged rocks at the end and made it to the top.

Standing beside my friend of nearly twenty years, I looked out at an endless mountain range holding two lakes from another world. Grant carved our initials into a rock, and I carved the word "sober" into another one. I was standing on top of the biggest sobriety cliché in the world: a mountain I had just climbed because I did it one step at a time. I was covered in mud, with cuts on my hands and arms, every breath a reminder that I wasn't getting the amount of oxygen my body needed. But I felt like the strongest person in the world— until a family with two preteens joined us at the top. Are the children out west on steroids, what the fuck?

Before I got sober I could tell you shady places to score drugs in shady areas of town. I liked my new travel recommendations better. If you're ever fortunate enough to end up at Lake Louise, go to the teahouse and order the best peppermint tea of your life.

That night on my drive to the show I watched the sun set over the prairies while I listened to the Tragically Hip's "Wheat Kings." In the past six months, I had seen New York City at sunset, the Atlantic Ocean at sunrise, fire-breathing jugglers on the crowded streets of Montreal, *The Starry Night* in the flesh at the Museum of Modern Art, and the top of Devil's Thumb looking down at God's creation. Those golden fields of wheat illuminated by the last rays of a sun casting shades of orange, yellow, blue, purple, and red that I'd never seen before may have been the most stunning sight of all.

I never thought I would say this, but it was better than pizza.

chapter 14

porn

I was the last of my friends to masturbate, and I thought I had
broken my penis when I came that first time. From my understanding, sperm was microscopic—so I assumed an invisible substance,
not unlike something out of a perverted episode of *The Magic School
Bus*, would leave my penis without a trace. I was scared that the
ejaculate was internal penis organ tissue or something and thought
I would have to go to the hospital for a broken wiener. But it felt so
good, I didn't care if I had broken it or not; I was willing to masturbate until I had no penis left. I got out of the bathtub, where I lay
fully clothed, cleaned up, and went downstairs to go on the internet.
One screeching robot orgy sound later, and I was on AskJeeves to
find out if I needed a new dick. Turns out, the only thing normal
about the experience *was* the ejaculate.

The soft-core porn that airs in Quebec after midnight is nothing
short of iconic in the Ottawa-Gatineau area. I've puffed and chugged
enough in my time to forget most of what I learned in the French
classes I took for eleven years, but I'll always remember the French
words for "blue" and "night." *Bleu Nuit* was the definition of appointment television for me when I was in grade eight.

"No, that's not real porn. This is real porn," the all-FUBU-clad teen told me.

A year later I was in my dad's basement and some of my brother's friends had brought a hard-core porn tape. It didn't scare the shit out of me, but it did scare the cum inside of me. The woman sounded like she was screaming in pain, and the guy was stepping on her neck while he was having sex with her. I'm not trying to kink-shame any-one who *wants* a foot slammed on them like they're a brake pedal when I say the event was jarring. After seeing that video, I thought all men had giant penises and all women enjoyed speaking directly into those penises like they were about to fight.

Now, anyone reading this who was born after 1999 must be thinking, *Soft-core? Hard-core? There's just porn. What is he talking about?*

You poor kids. Not only are we leaving you with a dying planet, but you think all mothers secretly want to show their daughters how to suck their boyfriend's dick properly.

After my education in my dad's basement about how minuscule my penis was I didn't watch porn again until two years later, when I was sixteen and already considered a binge alcoholic. I was mortified by my penis and my inability to be comfortable around women in any scenario that wasn't friendship. All my friends were having sex, and I didn't tell anybody, but even if a girl had wanted to, I wouldn't have been able to. I was afraid. I hated the sight of my own genitals and I could never see myself trusting anybody enough to be intimate with them.

I turned to porn for a lot of the same reasons I turned to drugs, and the similarities don't end there. When you're on hard drugs, you will check the time at two a.m., and thirty minutes later, the after-hours place kicks you out because it's almost noon. Watching porn creates similar rips in the space-time continuum where hours of your life evaporate in what feels like minutes. A conservative estimate of my time spent searching for and watching porn per week would be five hours. Which is 260 hours per year. Over fifteen years that works out to 3,900 hours. Factor in the time spent actually masturbating and that number skyrockets to 3,900.5 hours.

It's estimated to take 2,200 hours to learn fluent Chinese, 1,100 for Hindi, and 600 for Spanish. That totals 3,900 hours. I guess what I'm trying to say is: Can you imagine the amount of international porn I could have been watching without subtitles had I learned those languages? Wait, no. That's not the lesson to be learned from this. I've spent more of my time on this earth watching porn than I have reading books. It was the breast of times; it was the squirts of times. I got my first guitar around the time I started watching porn on a regular basis. If you wanna hear the worst version of "Smoke on the Water" of your life, just let me have three tries before I'll give up and say the guitar is out of tune. I'm supposed to be a writer, but I've spent more time on porn than I have on writing, and so very little of it counted as legitimate research.

Feeling shame after a particularly bad binge, using it to hide from bigger problems, trying to quit but not being able to, knowing it's not good for me in the long run but choosing the momentary pleasure it provides over all of the bad that comes with it—nearly all of the worst things about drugs and alcohol were present in my porn addiction. But it was more than that. I could browse through thousands of impossibly beautiful women before finally selecting the one I deemed to be wearing the sexiest outfit, saying the sexiest shit, and looking the most perfect. I would then return to the real world and expect to have realistic perceptions of a woman as a woman, or as a nurse/librarian/receptionist/teacher/yoga instructor ... you know, I could name pretty much any job.

I don't want to sound like a Bible-thumper; I just know that porn is bad for me. Just like if you can enjoy a glass of wine with dinner but stay in control and not let it ruin your life, I congratulate you and with my whole heart wish you nothing but that the fastest trains should run you over. If you are using pornography in a fashion you deem healthy, then by all means continue to defile your hard drive.

I was surprised to learn that my buddy Nathan was in the same boat as me. Incidentally, if you're in the porn-addict boat, I can't recommend rubber boots enough.

Nathan is from Canada's East Coast, and his dad wasn't around growing up either. He is a fan of professional wrestling and has never respected the social contract of an indoor voice. Nathan is the most likeable comedian I have ever seen, and he had the career I'd always dreamed of: he was living in New York, had just appeared on *Conan*, and was a regular at some of the biggest comedy clubs in the world. I couldn't even take part in the time-honoured comedian tradition of being jealous and bitter at your friend's successes because Nathan had worked himself to the bone and deserved everything he got.

In the more than ten years we'd known each other, I'd always thought Nathan was in complete control. He was driven and focused like a fighter. I didn't think anything ever tripped him up. I was wrong. We were both in Vancouver, and I had a week left of my tour when we sat down to talk for my podcast.

He was talking about porn when he said it, but Nathan could have been talking about booze, blow, smokes, weed, food, and any of the other things I was trying to fill this hole inside me with when he said, "None of that stuff is going to help anything if you're not happy with who it is that you are as a human being."

It's weird because I'd spent all those years using all that shit because I wasn't happy with who I was as a human being. Now that it was all gone, I was starting to be happy with who I was as a human being.

I was six months into the podcast, halfway to going the distance on quitting everything. The next day I dipped my hand into my second ocean, this time the Pacific. I flew home at the end of the month, concluding the longest tour of my life, which brought an end to my abstention from the most agonizing of all things I had been deprived of: Nora.

Now, I'll be the first to admit that being able to have regular sex while quitting porn is maybe the reason this book isn't being written by the lead prosecutor for my murder trial. However, quitting porn wasn't difficult, compared to my other vices, and I almost instantly felt all the benefits. I had more energy, time, and patience. Sex was more fulfilling in every way. I caught myself wanting to watch porn in the first few days, but the timing of the urges was what stood out—often, it was just out of pure boredom. I thought I knew, but I truly began to see how strong the similarities were between porn and my other addictions. Which made it easier to deal with, because by now I had all these tools to use. I started to play the tape out if I thought about watching porn. It never ended in me feeling great about myself and having a productive, clothing-unstained day.

Quitting porn was easy, but that didn't mean everything was. October wasn't just a struggle to make it through the podcast, it wasn't just a struggle to make it through sober—it was a struggle just to make it through.

The doctors still didn't have an answer for me about my attacks. By this point I had done blood tests, urine tests, EEGs, EKGs, and an MRI, and the results had all come back normal. I was having falls and tremors almost weekly, with the doctors befuddled as to the cause. There was a lot on my plate, and none of it was dairy or red meat. I would often become overwhelmed by the multiple cravings assaulting my discipline, as well as whatever it was that felt like it was taking over my body. I thought I had rewired that old thought out of my brain permanently, but it was creeping back in: *What if I'm like this forever?*

My last hope to figure out what was going on was a sleep test.

A burly and surly Russian technician duct-taped wires all over my body before he said, "Now, the head."

He scrubbed my scalp with a Brillo pad before slapping some goop on it and attaching the wires. After putting tubes in my nose and taping electrodes all over my face and body, the scariest man to ever tuck someone in said to me, "You sleep now," in a thick accent that must have originated in the Bond Villain province of Russia.

I was begging for them to tell me my problem was sleep apnea. Almost every male on my dad's side of the family has it, and it seemed like the obvious answer that had been right in front of me the entire time: that I stopped breathing so much at night for so long that my body and brain simply couldn't take it anymore. I had taken every medical test available and spent hours and hours in doctors' offices, wondering if I was going to die right when I most wanted to start living. It would all be over now—I'd just have to get a breathing machine for when I slept, and then I could move on with my life.

Most people don't want to hear "positive" when a doctor comes in with results, but that was the only thing I wanted to hear. I waited to hear that sweet word that would make this anguish finally end so I could get some help. I couldn't hear the other word, not again. I felt like either a bullet was going in my head or a bottle was going in my mouth if I heard that word one more time.

The doctor entered the room and pulled the trigger: "Negative."

• • •

"Positive, always. And you should think, like, good things are going to come, but you should go for it first. Don't wait for it. Don't stop. And never give up. Believe me now, good friends around you, good family, good people, they will help you. Don't take drugs. Don't, like, be alcoholic because that shit will not help you anymore."

My buddy Mo came on the podcast right when I needed him most.

As we sat down, we acknowledged we'd both come a long way. Mo had become a permanent resident of Canada and quit smoking a month ago. The interview was classic Mo, thoughtful, engaging, heartwarming, funny, and inspiring. Like so many times I'd talked to him, I had an epiphany. It happened as we signed off at the end of the interview.

"Thank you for inviting me," he said. "You're my big brother, and you know that. I love you so much."

Mo and I both had people we loved ripped away from us without warning, or even a chance to say goodbye. People who were family to us. It's easier in that situation to stop letting people into your heart, to give up. But if we had given up, we would have ended up losing a brother, too.

As the weather cooled that fall, the mysterious, undiagnosable illness invading my body began to pick up steam. I could barely walk at times, and I fell to the ground almost daily. I told Nora that I would break up with her if my symptoms didn't go away. I didn't want to drag her down with me.

But like I said to her in the hospital, Nora told me she wasn't going anywhere no matter what.

Regardless of my health problems, I had to be thankful. Because it was Thanksgiving, and that's, like, a rule or something. My family had painstakingly cooked me a separate holiday dinner without dairy products. Vienna and Annie were entranced by Nora. It was borderline cult-like, the way they took to her. Vienna, always a prisoner of the moment and never a slave to polite discourse, said to me by the end of the night, "Hey Alex, we like Nora better than you."

On Halloween Nora and I dressed up in matching children's size John Cena costumes. We danced for hours under strobe lights, sweating and stopping only to kiss. I felt high out of my fucking mind the entire night, yet I'd never been more sober.

When we ended up in my bed later that night, we got married, again. Every night before bed for months I'd been asking Nora to marry me, she'd say yes, and then we'd go to sleep as husband and wife. It was just a cute thing we did, but I knew I really did want to spend the rest of my life with her.

I had a lot of practice quitting things, and I had gained all of these ways to combat the temptations of my vices. Drinking lots of water, eating right, exercising, playing the tape out, feeling gratitude, recognizing things that were out of my control, and being aware of my thoughts. Because of all of these things, and having Nora in my life, quitting shit, including porn, was getting easier and easier.

chapter 15

credit cards

When your personal money manager is a tiny coked-up alcoholic who lives inside your head, you don't always get the soundest financial advice.

All right listen, up. We're in a bull market, but we don't need to buy a bull, so let's hit up the liquor store. Charge it. Okay, I'm hearing a lot of good things about the futures market right now, but if I've learned anything, it's to zig when they zag, so let's buy some cigarettes instead. Charge it. All right, now we're running low on alcohol again, and my sources are telling me there's a bar where we can get more. Charge it. Hey, someone here has Molly. Let's buy some by transferring money from our credit card to our chequing account. Interest? I don't find anything interesting about it, actually, ha ha. Old joke, don't worry about it. Let's just get these drugs inside of us and work out the fine print later. Shit, we already smoked that whole pack today? Supply and demand, let's go get another pack. What? This store doesn't take credit? I think you have that last ten in your pocket. Yes, there it is. Hey, look at us being responsible— we only spent ten dollars today. Let's Uber home.

I wasn't addicted to credit cards themselves, just to the way they got me the substances I was addicted to. My worst mind/life-altering benders wouldn't have been possible without my friend there to loan me the money, with a bit of interest, of course. I didn't even think of my credit card as real money; it just seemed like this magic wand that could grant me any substance I needed to put inside my body to bring me pleasure no matter how much trouble it caused. A get-into-jail-free card.

I thought of my credit card as a source of income, which is like thinking of a shark as a surfboard. It works for a bit, until it's feeding time.

"Hi, is this Mr Wood? I'm calling on behalf of Great White Financial. You owe us two fingers by next week or I'm afraid to say we're going to have to bite your face off."

The worst thing I would do was not even look at my statements. I was a child pulling the covers over my eyes because I was too scared to see the monster holding the receipt for a twenty-seven-dollar margarita. Credit cards symbolized the way I lived most of my life: putting something off in the moment to deal with later. Then, when later came, doing the bare minimum and putting off the rest until even later. The mistakes of the past were mounting and causing me stress, and the only thing that helped was making those same mistakes again. I was constantly trading a little easier today for a much harder tomorrow.

Credit cards were going to be the first item on my quit list with a contingency, though. All the bills linked to my credit card were still being paid, but that was it. No more spending money I didn't have. If I was going to make a purchase of any kind—a cab, a takeout meal, anything—it would be with my bank card or cash. Otherwise known as: money I already had.

Now, in boxing you aren't supposed to underestimate your opponent. That's how you end up getting knocked out in Tokyo by Buster Douglas. I was underestimating the power of credit cards, a road apple on my path to victory. I thought it would be easy to quit using credit cards, but I was wrong. It was even easier. I was on day 991 off cocaine, so day 1 off credit cards was, quite frankly, a joke.

There was just one challenge those first few days. One night, a cashier asked me how I wanted to pay for my dinner.

"Credit. No, wait. Cash," I said.

My friend Jeff is a talented comedian and producer who told me everything he knows about credit card debt when he sat down to do the podcast.

Jeff's marriage ended because he found out his wife was having an affair. He spiralled into a haze of alcohol, cigarettes, fried food, and a $27,000 debt. A lot of people don't get back up after going through something like that. There are a lot of factors, both internal and external, that go into quitting drugs, getting into shape, getting out of debt, getting out of bed, or changing your life. I've done my best to pull at your heartstrings talking about the emotional perseverance that's needed to beat addiction, but Jeff revealed the biggest factor of all, the one thing above all else that has to happen if you're going to change who you are for the better. You can sit back from the edge of your chair because it's not a secret. You know it already.

When I asked Jeff how he paid off the money he owed, he said, "I just fucking buckled down and hammered *everything* I had into it."

When you do that, a tiny piece of plastic seems like just that.

chapter 16

gossip

With every step he takes, his condition worsens. His staff doesn't hit the ground with the same command and confidence of his earlier years, when he freed slaves and parted seas. Now it comes to a rest so gentle, so as to not disturb even the dust on the ground. After forty years of wandering the harsh desert, Moses has reached the summit of Mount Sinai. Storm clouds suddenly race and form overhead and a bolt of lightning rains down from the heavens, alighting a nearby bush with a flame too bright for mortal eyes to look at directly. A voice pours forth that is so unlike anything ever heard before that it must be divine.

It's a famous biblical moment, when God gives Moses the laws that will govern humanity and, if followed, lead to eternal salvation at the right hand of the Lord. But something the book of Exodus leaves out is that two of my ancestors are hiding behind a large boulder, unseen while God dictates the Ten Commandments to Moses.

"Thou shalt not murder," the booming voice instructs.

Moses nods, along with my hiding forebears.

"Thou shalt not steal."

My ancestors can't believe their good fortune at witnessing this iconic moment.

"Thou shalt not bear false witness against thy neighbour," God says.

"Oh, that reminds me, did I tell you thy neighbour went out of town and I saw thy other neighbour's donkey parked out front all weekend? You didn't hear it from thy, but I'm pretty sure there was a lot more than coveting going on," my ancestor says before taking a bong hit.

If you don't have anything nice to say about someone, you shouldn't say anything at all ... to them. Say it to me, behind their back, instead. I've always got an ear to lend for some slander. I will think of the person I'm going to tell your secret to while I'm telling you I won't tell anyone.

Is gossip addictive? Of course not! It goes way beyond addiction. It's been hard-wired into our brains since we started making noise.

Dr Michael Corballis is a psychologist who specializes in the nature and evolution of language. Dr Corballis and I have a long-standing working relationship where we have access to each other's research files and summer homes. In his 2011 book, *The Recursive Mind: The Origin of Human Language, Thought, and Civilization,* Corballis writes, "I think that grammatical language evolved primarily to enable us to share episodes ... Language is exquisitely designed to communicate 'who did what to whom, ... where, when and why.'"

Whereas other primates had calls or signals to warn of a predator or to announce fertility, humans transformed our verbal noises into complicated speech so as to communicate about things that aren't directly in front of us, the non-present. While a chimpanzee would make a screeching noise to alert the other chimps that a giant snake was in their territory this very second, it never developed a way to communicate that a giant snake was in their territory last week and seems to always slither up this one tree. Gossip, in its primitive form, was an absolute necessity for staying alive. The earliest gossip functioned to protect us from predators or dangerous situations. In the modern Western world, however, gossip is no longer about warning of sabre-toothed tigers; it's about ridiculing bleach-toothed cougars.

I'll leave it there without diving into whether gossip was a form of social grooming and whether our language evolved from an auditory function or gestures. If you would like to hear my thoughts on those matters, be on the lookout for my next book, *Evolutionary Gossip: From Throwing Shit to Talking It.*

For my purposes, I'm defining gossip as saying anything bad about anyone I know. It might not sound that difficult to give up gossip, but I almost decided to put it as the last thing to quit because I thought it was going to be so hard. I was constantly saying the things I hate about the people I love. The only prompting it took was when the listener had to prompt me to stop talking because the café was closing. There were a lot of similarities between drugs and gossip for me: I didn't think of the consequences before engaging in it, I didn't concern myself with whom I may hurt because of it, and I didn't seem to ever reach a limit where I felt satisfied. But the biggest similarity that I noticed was this: in the moment it may have felt good, but after it was done I felt worse than I had before I started.

As per usual, I was tested in my first couple of days after quitting gossip. I was on the phone with a friend and a familiar punching bag of ours came up in conversation, someone we mutually spent entirely too much of our fleeting time shitting on.

I felt the impulse to trash this person to my friend, but it moved so slowly, and the speed at which I played the tape out to counter it was supersonic: I spend twenty minutes trashing someone until another person comes up, and then I drop another twenty minutes of my life going over their faults instead of working on my own. Suddenly, I'm nearly an hour deep into a conversation that has been nothing but toxicity and has added nothing to my life. Most importantly, why am I this emotional over something that isn't even about me?

All these thoughts happened in the amount of time it took my brain to tell my mouth to open. I closed my mouth, cleared my throat, and changed the subject.

I expected to struggle with quitting gossip because of the ramifications it would have on my mental well-being. I needed to vent the anger inside me, or it would explode. I also felt like not gossiping made me vulnerable somehow. Constantly saying bad shit about people reminded me to keep my guard up. I thought every time I would pass up an opportunity to degrade someone, I would make myself weaker and more open to being hurt.

But that day in early December when I closed my mouth and changed the subject I didn't feel like I was going to explode. I felt quite the opposite. A feeling that I wish were less fleeting. I felt safe.

• • •

"Close your eyes," Zac said.

My brother and I have seen our relationship bounce between brothers and enemies since we were kids. Over the years we have apologized for various betrayals and assaults to become closer than ever. I began to seek out his counsel and he mine. I love him, and we both put in a lot of time and effort to wind up brothers in more than name alone. But that doesn't mean I am ever going to trust that piece of shit when he tells me to close my eyes.

"I'm not closing my eyes," I said forcefully.

"Just close them," he said. "It's a birthday present. I promise."

I was unmoved by his blatant attempt at deception. My "present" was most assuredly some kind of strike to my testicles.

"Close your eyes. It's a surprise," the rest of my family urged.

I began to weigh the possibility of whether my thirty-two-year-old brother would actually convince me to close my eyes so he could punch me in the balls, on my birthday, while my family was watching.

"I'm not closing my eyes, fucker," I snapped.

After I told my family I was coming for all of them if this ended up being a trick, I gave in and closed my eyes, while covering my crotch with both hands.

"We're all so proud of you for getting sober," my brother said. "You're a champion, and champions need a belt."

I opened my eyes to see my brother holding a replica wrestling championship belt. I ripped my shirt in half, put the belt around my waist, and told my family if they wanted my title, they were going to have to come take it from me this Sunday in a steel cage.

On my thirty-first birthday, I celebrated two years off alcohol, and on New Year's Eve, I was booked to do one of the biggest shows of my career. The best thing I did that holiday season was something I had been putting off for a long time, always moving it to the back burner, while getting fucked up stayed on the front burner. My friend Graham and I finally organized a Q&A for amateur comedians in the city, and admittance was by donation of clothing or food for the Ottawa Mission. Only seven people showed up, but they brought enough donations to pack an entire van.

I always considered myself a charitable person because I had thoughts of charity. I considered myself a noble person because I had thoughts of nobility. A good person because I had thoughts of doing good. But if people were their thoughts, you'd be reading this under a bridge in secret because far-right conspiracy theorist Alex Jones had conquered the world, and then banned gay frogs and books. The point is, you are your actions, not how you think of yourself. I didn't think of myself as a bad person, even with my known penchant for stealing famous quotations and passing them off as my own. But wasn't it I who said, "The only thing necessary for the triumph of evil is for good men to do nothing"?

I was done with doing drugs, but I was also done with doing nothing.

● ● ●

The last thing I told you about Wafik was that the first time I saw him after quitting drinking he said he didn't know if he could be friends with me anymore. What I didn't tell you is that he quit drinking, too, not long after that conversation. We went from being each other's enablers to being each other's supporters. To the shock of everyone who knew us, we both quit cocaine, alcohol, weed, and cigarettes. Now Wafik got to see his daughter way more, and he'd just had a son.

Both our roads to sobriety had been paved in relapses. On my podcast over Christmas, Wafik revealed the thought process behind his: "Because you quit, you think you can quit again."

It was the same thing I did, and I'm sure a lot of addicts think the same way. It's the kind of illogical, paradoxical notion that sounds reasonable when you're an addict. Thinking that you're so good at not having cocaine that you can have cocaine. I was glad neither of us was falling for that anymore. And I was happy to have my comedy dad back.

● ● ●

In my mother's basement that holiday season, old habits crept in. Why? Because I was bored. I know it's not the most inspiring reason, but it's the truth. Boredom is frequently cited as a reason for relapsing, and it's been an old standby of mine. I just decided to go in a different direction with my boredom that Christmas and wrote something instead. In the same basement where I used to drunkenly do cocaine, I wrote an essay on quitting my addictions.

Then I went back to Toronto for my last show of the year.

"You do look cool," comedy icon Robert Klein said as he adjusted my lapels backstage at the historic Massey Hall before my set in front of 3,000 people, including Nora and her mom.

I couldn't believe how different my body felt after only thirty days off gossip. I had always thought of gossip as letting it out. Now I saw that it was more like letting gossip in. Letting it into my body. It was just like alcohol—what I thought was helping me was actually hurting me.

At midnight, I kissed Nora, and I kissed sugar goodbye.

chapter 17

sugar

"Drinking a sugar solution on an intermittent schedule can promote sugar bingeing and cause signs of dependence while releasing dopamine repeatedly like a drug of abuse."
—PRINCETON UNIVERSITY

"Available evidence in humans shows that sugar and sweetness can induce reward and craving that are comparable in magnitude to those induced by addictive drugs."
—UNIVERSITÉ DE BORDEAUX

Look, if your jaw just dropped to the floor because you're hearing for the first time that sugar isn't good for us, I have more bad news for you. We don't have flying cars by the year 2000 and R. Kelly's music will age horrifyingly.

There isn't a universal consensus on sugar being addictive in the same way as drugs. I have only my anecdotal evidence to submit:

• My brain is nothing but pleasure while I am consuming sugar.

- There is a comedown, with shame and sadness, from sugar that is not dissimilar to the comedown from hard drugs.
- I will binge on sugar until I am in physical pain that lasts for hours.
- I know all these consequences but still put it inside my body.
- But in times I was in withdrawal from hard drugs, if you said to me, "I know what you mean, I haven't had sugar in a week," I would have bitten you several times on the face and neck.

Although the intensity of the physical withdrawal symptoms is more severe with drugs, a lot of aspects of quitting sugar are harder. Social acceptance is a major one; after all, there isn't a bell that rings signalling everyone in the neighbourhood to run with glee because the opium truck is here. The bride and groom at a wedding don't laugh and pose for pictures as they shove magic mushrooms into each other's faces.

Another challenge sugar presents is that our bodies need food, and our brains are evolutionarily wired to eat more than we need to because we didn't always know when our next meal was coming. Outside of the 1980s, there is no evidence to suggest we have an evolutionary need to consume cocaine.

Sugar can play tricks on your mind. When you eat food, your brain gets a hit of dopamine. And a piece of cake gives you way more than a kale amount. Your brain likes dopamine, so it wants more, which is also how drugs work. At the same time, your blood sugar spikes, so your brain tells your body to make more insulin to lower the blood sugar. Do you know what happens when your blood sugar drops? You get hungry. All the while, millions of years of evolution have left an ape screaming at you to eat as much cake as possible.

I weighed more than 200 pounds on New Year's Day, the heaviest I had been in years. Over Christmas I'd put on almost fifteen pounds while eating anything that was unhealthy without red meat or dairy in it. I had been jumping from rock to rock with the bad things I put in my body. There were no more rocks left. The rules were: no sugar, no white starches, no food in packaging.

I had eggs with veggies for breakfast; a vegan, sugar-free protein shake for lunch; and for dinner, chicken with chickpeas—and an old adversary of mine. I despised broccoli but forced it into my body. Day one passed without so much as a bother. I also may not have noticed because I was homing in on finishing my anti-boredom Christmas project.

What I experienced on day two off refined sugar was not a headache. No—what happened was my head was triple-booked by the running of the bulls, a contest to see which marching band could blow up the most dynamite, and my father watching television. Only withdrawal can make me feel listless and exhausted at the same time. Physically, those day two sugar withdrawal symptoms were as bad as anything I'd ever had.

Two things made that first week easier: Nora made me a dairy-free, sugar-free chicken alfredo that was—and I'm not being delusional when I say this—delicious. The other thing was that my article came out.

The boredom I'd felt over Christmas eventually manifested in my article called "How to Quit Everything in 2018," which was published by *Vice*. It boosted my downloads enough to put the podcast on the iTunes chart for the first time. I got more emails and DMs than ever from people telling me my words helped them in some way. A few people told me they had recently relapsed when my piece inspired them to give sobriety another shot. I didn't know it at the time, but even a producer at NBC read it.

A comedian named Charlie I'd eaten poutine with at Just for Laughs in 2009 also read it. He asked me if I'd ever thought about writing a book.

All because I was bored.

I was trying to rewire my brain to not think of boredom as some egg timer that goes off to let me know it's time to get drunk, watch porn, or eat a duffle bag filled with ice cream.

My old friend K. Trevor knows all about rewiring your brain. Teddy bears describe other nicer teddy bears as "just a big K. Trev." He's the only act I've ever seen that made me think, *Well, he's gonna be famous for sure one day*. He'd had a momentous couple of years—he was one of the stars of the hit series *Letterkenny*, appeared on *Jimmy Kimmel Live!*, let me stay on his couch when I relapsed last fall without a pot to piss in, and was a regular at all the major festivals. He was also diagnosed with type 2 diabetes and came on the podcast to talk about coping with it.

"It's a pain in the ass," he said. "It's just changing your habits, from doing all the unhealthy stuff to forcing yourself—and for a while, you are forcing yourself—to be better."

Everyone's "for a while" is different, but he was right. You are going to have to force yourself in the beginning of making a change.

It worked for K. Trev because he cut out almost all sugar and alcohol, and lost eighty pounds, and his last blood test came back as above average health on the glucose meter, meaning he doesn't have diabetes anymore. When you force yourself in the beginning, you won't have to live the rest of your life forcing yourself to do the right thing, as K. Trev knew all too well.

"I'm a peanut butter fanatic, and I always hated natural peanut butter. We always had regular peanut butter at my place, but we'd go to my aunt's place and she'd always have natural peanut butter. You'd sit there with a knife, like stirring the oil in, and then if you don't do it right, at the end of the fucking container, you don't have enough oil left anymore, so it's dry and shit. But I'll tell you, when your doctor says you have to—now I love natural peanut butter. Now I love stirring that oil in, like, that oil means I can eat it."

The next day, I threw up on the treadmill at the gym. I hadn't exercised in six weeks, my body wasn't used to the extra weight, and I didn't want to be there. But I forced myself. The next day I went because I wanted to. It only took a few more trips before I got my legs and cardio back. Turns out you can't ruin years of hard work with a few bad weeks. I had a savings account for the first time in my life, and the $1,500 in it was the exact same number the app on my phone told me I had saved from not smoking cigarettes over the last six months. I was coming up on three years off cocaine, and it was over a year since I'd touched anything harder than weed (which I was nine months off, too).

I felt so good, I signed up for getting punched in the face.

My first organized fight would be in April, a little over a year after I'd started my podcast. Three neurologists had now told me with absolute medical certainty that there was nothing wrong with my brain, structurally speaking. They said I should seek a different kind of help. I thought I could find the answers I needed in the ring. I had confidence I could win. After all, maybe I wasn't Robinson or Leonard, but I could beat sugar.

chapter 18

social media

Stay with me because this is going to get weird for a second.

Equation A:

50 × 4.4 million = 220 million

220 million × 52 = 11.4 billion

Equation B:

2 × 2.77 billion = 5.4 billion

5.4 billion × 365 = 1.9 trillion

The result of one of those equations is the number of hours combined humanity spent on the Apollo missions over eleven years. The other is the number of hours combined humanity spent on social media in 2019 alone. Hint: If you want to know which one is higher, it's the depressing answer.

For all the teachers, I'll show my work.

The Apollo space program ran for eleven years. At its peak there were 400,000 people working on it, but for our purposes we'll say that was the number working every year. Let's say every single one of them was working fifty hours a week, every week, every year, because they thought they could be promoted to first astronaut to walk on the moon/upper management. That's 11.4 billion hours.

It was estimated that in 2019 there were 2.77 billion social media users in the world. GlobalWebIndex reports that, worldwide, users spend an average of two hours and twenty-two minutes online daily. Let's round that down to two hours, just to be safe.

If the difference between trillions of hours and billions of hours is too hard to conceptualize, combine those hours and put it into years, and a clearer picture develops. From 1961 to 1972, humans spent 1.3 million years working on sending twelve people to the moon. In 2019 alone, we spent 219 million years on social media. One giant leap for humankind turned into one giant tweet for man-likes. What could we have done with that time if we'd had our priorities straight? Or: How many dank memes could NASA have come up with had they not been bogged down with the Apollo missions?

When I open my phone or computer I always check social media. Always. Interesting article about how to battle climate change? That was inspiring. I will write those letters to parliament—right after I see what people from high school think about pineapple on pizza. Checking the score of a Raptors game? Better check what strangers who haven't played organized sports think about this. My entire family has been kidnapped and the abductors are asking for an online money transfer to be sent in the next thirty seconds or everyone dies? Imagine how many likes a ransom note would get, though.

Social media does the same thing to me as cigarettes: it makes me think it has the answer to my problems, while the only solution it ever seems to offer is more consumption of *it*, which in turn leads to more problems. As with sugar, I'm not going to get into whether it is a pathological addiction. I just know I've spent thousands of hours using social media—and for the most part liking myself less with every like.

The internet and social media are a juxtaposition cesspool of ignorance and beauty. For instance, I find it helps my writing process to play classical music in the background. At this exact moment I'm writing this while listening to a YouTube video entitled "6 Hours of Mozart for Studying, Concentration, Relaxation." Below are unedited, I-promise-you-completely-real comments posted under the video:

I take issue with people who listen to Mozart as "background music." Really? How do you think Mozart would feel about that? Personally, I don't see how you could do it. I came into the room and the final movement of the Jupiter was playing—totally captivating—and then into the 23rd piano concerto—the most brilliant and engaging piece of music written. How can one focus on "trigonometry" or anything else and not give one's full attention to Mozart?

I listen to Mozart as "background music," it doesn't mean I don't enjoy listening to it lol, that's not an issue. Being able to focus on studies and not on Mozart is an accomplishment. It is better than to listen to other people rambling/making noise. That's why I call it "study music" because it helps me focus xD

Do you imply that i am not that civilized otherwhile, you treble clef?
STFU NO1 Carez
Einstein was a shill, fraud and pedophile

This is what the internet, social media, and online sharing culture has given us. The gift of Mozart's most compelling piano sonatas compiled into a six-hour medley that is available for free in seconds. That and Albert Einstein truthers. E = STFUNO1Carez[2].

Your narrator has been known to be dragged into his fair share of online disagreements. If I'm being honest, it's less "dragged" than "dove in headfirst." It's also probably more "lion's share" than "fair share." Oh, also less "disagreements" and more like "made derogatory comments about the physical appearance of anti-vaxxers." I will start and end my day with a fight online. I say start and end because, just like how I used drugs, once I start there is no stopping. When I start my day with those vices I'm also effectively ending it.

The language of social media is similar to that of drug culture. They even call us users. But the creepiest term is also widely accepted in everyday language and not even seen as weird anymore. I don't care how good a dealer's shit was, I would never buy off them if they called their customers followers. That's some Jonestown-level acid right there.

Social media wasn't something I was planning on quitting entirely forever for two reasons. One, like so many things in comedy, you have to pull a *Godfather* and accept it as part of "the business we've chosen." Two, a necessary evil doesn't have to be necessarily evil. I enjoy being connected with family and old friends on social media. I've been exposed to great causes and art because of it. But I can't keep losing days of my life scrolling Facebook and Instagram. I'll have to learn to take it in moderation. Especially so I can use it to reach out to future podcast guests, like Mike MacDonald.

The King of Canadian Comedy would be my last interview, in two months, for the podcast finale. Mike was supposed to be dead years ago, but he'd made a comeback more miraculous than I'd ever seen in a boxing ring. Instead of dying, he'd started killing again.

• • •

I talked so much about the how, why, when, and where of my poop habits on my podcast that traditional academia might reject a lot of my hypotheses. However, I submit my podcast guest from early February, Allie, as a case study in textbook addict thinking:

"I feel like there's so much insecurity and it's rooted in yourself. I feel insecure about myself, so I want to use. You get a rush of dopamine every time you use, so you feel a little better, and then all of a sudden you're feeling insecure about yourself again. So maybe then you feel like you need to use again, and then you do it and it's a cycle. But it's rooted in the insecurity. By the end of it, it's magnified that insecurity."

Allie and I also talked about the tolerance that builds up, leading to chasing the dragon, and the insatiable appetite that grows from there. Obviously, we talked about the cravings in the first few days off. Allie also talked about how she got in touch with healthier methods of dealing with her problems. This was all pretty basic stuff that I would go so far as to say an overwhelming majority of addicts in recovery can relate to. That about covers Allie's episode.

Oh wait, I almost forgot to tell you what she quit. It was Snapchat.

With only two months left for my podcast, and my quit list, I considered my will to be made of iron. I thought social media was sort of cute, in a "Look at you, trying to prove you're addictive," kind of way. But then I woke up that first morning off social media and my brain told me as soon as it turned on: "Grab your phone and check Facebook."

It was less cute when I had the same thought thirty seconds later. By lunch, I'd decided to keep track of the number of times I had the impulse to check social media. It wasn't just the impulses that mimicked substance withdrawal; it was the letdown in my brain when it remembered it wasn't going to get a hit of dopamine. They weren't physical cravings, so they were easier to deal with in that way, but the sheer number of these impulses was challenging. That first day, my brain told me to check social media forty-eight times, including right before I went to sleep.

• • •

I had just crossed off three years off cocaine and almost three weeks off social media when I got the email.

Hi Alex,

I am working on an upcoming series on addictions for NBC's Megyn Kelly Today *and came across your podcast. Could I give you a call this afternoon?*

That email was almost all the words I'd ever wanted said to me. If the name was Letterman or O'Brien and the words "addictions" and "today" were replaced with "comedians" and "tonight."

"We saw your *Vice* article and we loved it," the NBC News producer said on the other end of the phone.

Even the parts about shitting? I thought.

"It led us to your podcast, and we loved it as well."

Even the parts about shitting? I thought, again.

Seriously, why was I getting a phone call from NBC News about *Alex Wood Quits Everything*?

Below is a list of things I had said on my podcast:

- "Fuck me with your beak, future bird."
- "Refined sugar has been linked to terrorism."
- "I really would have loved to have bathed in and drank this young man's blood, though. That would've given me great pleasure."
- "By scanning the brains of compulsive porn users with an MRI, while they view erotic images, you know, of your mom."
- "I watched *27 Dresses* and I don't want to make this a movie review podcast, but by the time she gets to that twenty-eighth dress, your heart will fucking melt."
- "You can't help but look up and just think, 'Wow, I wonder how big that thing's dick must have been.'"
- "If you're going to jerk off to this, you're a real weird person."
- "That's my new nickname by the way, Alex 'Hot Cock' Wood."

I guess I didn't mention my genitals or murder during the phone call because they booked me a trip to New York to be on the show. Chet Huntley was the NBC news anchor who told America that

President Kennedy had been killed, and now I would be on an NBC news program to tell America that it feels just as good when I cum sober. Really, though, how serious could they be about the whole "news" thing if they had Megyn "All Lives Matter" Kelly on it?

After I told Nora and my family my good news, a sinking feeling set in. It didn't take me long to figure out what it was: I couldn't brag about this on social media. Sure, it would be a good career move to get this out there—but it was more than that. I couldn't kid myself anymore that social media had its claws in me based solely on a need to further my career. I missed the continuous hits of dopamine that got delivered to my brain all day when I posted something that got a lot of likes. I knew the feeling well, so I knew what I missed most of all was chemical.

But there was a feeling that quickly replaced the sinking one, and it was excitement. Something about the date sounded familiar when NBC was making the arrangements. I wanted to stay in New York for a whole week and maybe do some comedy shows, but I had this nagging feeling that I already had plans. That's right, I realized I was supposed to watch the Wilder versus Ortiz fight with Dylan. No big deal, there would be other fights, and other times to watch Dylan cry. I'd watch it in New York; after all, there must be a place in a city this big that shows the—*Oh my fucking God, the fight is happening in New York!* If you're like me and you find yourself in New York City six days before a world heavyweight title fight, you go.

The first time I had arrived in New York it was on a Greyhound bus. Ten months later I was outside LaGuardia Airport looking at a man in a suit standing in front of one of those SUVs for presidents or Instagram stars and holding a placard with my name on it. Then he dropped me at my hotel in the heart of Manhattan, where I had a room overlooking the city. I had set such high expectations for everything at Just for Laughs in the summer to be perfect, including myself, and I didn't want to let that happen again. Even if I wasn't there to perform comedy, and even if I was being interviewed by a journalist whose most impassioned political stance is that Santa is in fact white, I was there. I started this podcast by myself in my bedroom, and now I was skating laps on this famous ice rink. I'd seen it a million times onscreen, but I just couldn't stop looking up at 30 Rockefeller Plaza, thinking of all the legendary comedians, actors, and musicians that had gone into that building before me. I only had three days left before I would quit my smartphone, so I took some pictures before I went back to my hotel and went to sleep.

The next morning I couldn't help myself. I should have been professional and just gone to hair and makeup, but instead, I asked if it was okay to take a detour along the way. I stuck my head into the *Tonight Show* studio, and even empty there was an energy in the air. I was about twenty feet from the stage. If this interview went well, maybe I could get closer one day.

The *Today Show* shoots multiple episodes and segments Monday morning, to be aired the rest of the week, but it's the same studio audience across the board. One of the segments shooting before mine was about therapy puppies that were given as a surprise to soldiers who had just returned home from overseas. That's what I was following. This audience was going from impossibly adorable puppies given to wounded veterans to a foreigner who didn't do cocaine anymore.

I was waiting in the wings when Megyn Kelly walked up to me, shook my hand, thanked me for being on the show, excused herself, and then stood five feet away from me, staring forward, waiting for us to get called on set. Within minutes, I was facing the hundreds in the studio audience, and the red light on the camera turned on.

"I'll give you the last word on advice to others," Megyn Kelly said before we wrapped up.

"If you want to quit anything, just do it," I said. "It sounds so simplistic, but we give ourselves these excuses, and we always justify why we're doing things, but you really have to want to quit something, and you have to hold yourself accountable. That's what I would say, and also, reach out for help."

"Well, said. Thank you." Megyn Kelly sounded so solemn. And then she turned to the camera and said cheerfully, "What does your doodle say about you? We have a doodle expert that's going to analyze audience members' doodles and maybe even one of mine. After this."

I left 30 Rock and told myself I had to get back there one day.

Forty-eight hours later, the segment aired, and forty-eight hours and six minutes later, I was pacing in front of a liquor store.

● ● ●

"Welcome to episode forty-seven of *Alex Wood Quits Everything*. It's February 28th. I am on day 334 off of weed, day 304 off of caffeine, day 273 off of biting my nails, day 243 off of cigarettes, day 212 off of red meat, day 181 off of dairy, day 151 off of porn, day 151 off of cigars, day 121 off of credit cards, day 90 off of gossip, day 59 off of sugar, day 28 off of social media. The last episode's intro was coming to you from a beautiful hotel room overlooking downtown Manhattan across the street from Radio City Music Hall and 30 Rockefeller Plaza. And this intro is in a really grimy Airbnb in Brooklyn.

"Today really crystallized that I need professional help. I watched the *Today Show* segment and I just thought I looked like a fat loser as soon as I saw it. And then I thought that I sounded stupid, sanctimonious, and dull. I felt like I was having a panic attack watching it. It was the longest five and a half minutes of my life, watching this segment. Uh, I truly felt like I was gonna cry watching it. I just fucking hated it so much. As soon as the segment was done I thought, like, 'Fuck it, I'm going to go on a bender. I fucking hate myself and I need some kind of escape.' I got all the way to the front door of the corner store, decided I'd think about it a little bit more. I didn't want to make the decision to relapse so rashly, and I just started pacing around on the street. I'm getting texts from my mom and my dad and my family and my friends about how much they love this segment. And that was making me feel even worse.

"I didn't relapse because—I can't lie, it wasn't for myself—I didn't want to disappoint my family and my friends and people who listen to the podcast, and that's fucked up. It should have been for myself, and I should have not been so miserable watching the *Today Show* segment. So I realized that I really need some help, and I can't keep doing this by myself. And I don't mean the podcast.

"I really did consider earlier today scoring some booze and some cigarettes and some weed. I knew it wouldn't solve my problems. That's the fucked-up thing. I was playing the tape out: Me passed out in Brooklyn. This wasn't going to make my problems go away, and I shouldn't be doing this. And I didn't care for a second. I knew all of it. It feels like you're in a forest and your demons are trying to hunt you the fuck down, and drugs and alcohol can help you hide from those demons. But it's a pretty shitty hiding spot that they provide you. Those big scary demons are gonna find you through the forest anyway. I'm gonna end this intro by saying I am proud of myself. For today, not for the *Today Show*."

I fought back tears the entire time I was recording that intro as the smell of weed filled the air from the next room over in my Airbnb. There were lots of reasons watching the interview hit me so hard I almost didn't get back up. I'm filled with a burning self-hatred whenever I watch myself on film—that was the ice cream in this sadness sundae. The highest point of my career being sitting in a chair across from one of Fox News's most popular all-time on-air personalities? That was the chocolate sauce. Being, literally, twenty feet from my dreams was just the cherry on top.

Deep down, I was hoping this would be it. The pain would finally stop. The self-loathing, the distrust, the night terrors, and the times something would set me off and all I could think of for days would be killing myself. Turns out Megyn Kelly doesn't have that kind of power, so I thought a bottle might.

Three nights ago, skating on the rink outside Rockefeller Center, my sobriety felt as solid as the ice beneath me. That feeling was, in no small way, related to the podcast interview I had just done. Ian Fidance is a hilarious, inspiring comedian I'd met outside one of the clubs when I came to New York ten months before, and we instantly bonded over comedy and sobriety. Ian was one of the people I knew the least going into our interview, but by the end I felt like he knew me better than people I'd known for years.

It was hard not to after he said, "I ain't the only person that's happened to, but the booze was always the best thing because then I could concentrate on why I gotta get sober. 'Man, I gotta work on my sobriety. I can't address these other things.' You know what I mean? You can always just make that the whipping boy of all your problems. 'Well, I'm this way because I'm an alcoholic, man. I got to concentrate on my sobriety.' You know, that's such a good out for everything. And then you don't focus on your next year. It's a false pat on the back, you know? 'Hey, I was sober today,' instead of, like, getting deep down, reaching in that garbage. It's just saved my life, changed my life."

That was what I had been doing my entire life. It's easy to explain, really. Being an addict whose life is constantly in shambles is easier to deal with than that garbage. I knew I couldn't duck it much longer. I was going to have to reach into the garbage soon.

Near the end of our interview Ian said something else that I'll take with me forever. "I'm supposed to be in a fucking gutter right now. I should be dead, man. You should be fucking dead. You shouldn't be here. You should be fucking dead, not here."

I had always focused on the good things that I "should be" but wasn't. I'd never considered the bad things that I "should be" and wasn't. All the nights I'd spent going to sleep with the lights on because I was scared that if I turned them off I would overdose and die. The times I'd felt suicidal.

I should be dead, I realized.

I didn't think hearing that I should be dead could ever make me feel so alive.

After the podcast, we went outside and kept talking like the interview had never ended. Chronologically, this chapter should end with my near relapse, but instead, I'm choosing to end it with Ian and me. Because if you told your friends you saw it, they wouldn't believe you. There was an impossible sight on the streets of Manhattan that night. Dead men walking.

chapter 19

smartphone

Gather around the fireplace channel, younger readers. I have a tale to tell. About something I've seen with my own eyes and heard with my own ears, from a bygone era long forgotten. At the very end of the 1900s was when I first remember seeing them in everyday life. Before that, it was only in movies. They were even at my junior high school. Not many of them, but enough to notice. A human being stood out so prominently back then if they had one in their hand. The rest of us would gaze on and marvel, "What kind of asshole thinks they need a cellphone?"

It's true, I swear. We may not admit it, but when cellphones first came out of action movies and into real life, we hated them. The idea of needing to be reached twenty-four hours a day was reserved for only the Batmanniest of jobs. But somewhere along the way, we all decided, or it was decided for us, that we were important enough to be literally on call at all times.

After a while, that was cool and all, but wouldn't it be great to be able to talk to someone without having to go through the gruelling task of talking to someone? Texting brought with it new and exciting ways for human beings to show each other their genitals and kill each other while driving.

Then you know what they did to these tiny contraptions? They made them smart. Smart enough that communicating with another person wasn't even necessary for using the phone. For the first time ever, you didn't need another human being on the other end. All you needed to interact with was the phone itself.

During the rise of mobile cellular devices, some people began to wonder if it was safe to have these things that emit radio-frequency electromagnetic waves near our brains and reproductive organs at all hours.

"Of course they're safe," said cellphone companies.

"We aren't sure," said scientists.

"We are sure," retorted the unbiased cellphone companies with nothing to gain.

"Excessive cellphone use has been linked to a variety of health problems, both physical and psychological," said the virgins.

"Name one."

"Eye strain!"

"That could be from all the tablets and laptops."

"Don't you guys make those, too?"

"Next question."

"These aren't questions, but okay. Excessive cellphone use has created a new health problem called text neck."

"Text neck! That could be from anything."

"Infertility in men."

"You know, a lot of people are just adopting dogs now."

"One in six cellphones have fecal matter on them."

"Oh, like you never eat at McDonald's?"

And those were just the physical problems presented by Severely Needing a Keypad Experience, or SNAKE, which was named after the cellphone program (we didn't even call them apps yet) I believe was the precursor to all the attention-draining and dopamine-firing apps that would follow. It was the first thing about phones I remember people using the term "addictive" for. Released in 1997, Snake was a game on 350 million devices at its peak. Simplistic and intricate at the same time, it engrossed an entire generation. The game consisted of controlling a snake that gets bigger every time it feeds, to the point it's so big it can't avoid eating its own tail and dying. It's like it was sent back in time to warn us all about what was to come with smartphones.

SNAKE's physical problems are paired with awful psychological ones. According to Kent State University, after a survey of 454 students ranked them in order of their cellphone use into three groups, from High User (reported ten hours of use per day) to LUE (Low Use Extrovert, three hours of use per day), the HUs were the most "susceptible to boredom" and "experienced the most distress," while the LUEs were reported as having the "highest preference for challenge, most aware, least susceptible to boredom." Obviously, after seeing the results of a study like this, one can't help but ponder—wait, three hours a day is the low user?

SNAKE has also been linked to relationship problems. In a comprehensive study done right now in my book I can prove it. Think of a time when a romantic partner's cellphone use upset you. That didn't take long, did it? You thought of that instantly. More than one instance, probably. Oh, nothing came to mind? That's so cool. Why don't you call your parents who are still together and talk about how fucking annoyingly healthy you are in all of your interpersonal relationships?

Somehow the links between SNAKE and depression, anxiety, sleep disorders, and a slew of other problems aren't even the worst part. Those problems take a back seat to the biggest issue. And it's a good thing for those problems because that's the safest place to be in a crash, and a lot of drivers out there are texting. Texting and driving has been a major worldwide health hazard for ten years now.

According to United Nations statistics, 1.25 million people die worldwide in car crashes every year. Various studies across the globe have put the number of car accident fatalities where cellphone use is the cause at anywhere from fifteen percent to twenty-seven percent. Let's go with twenty percent. When applied to the number of car accident fatalities worldwide, we find 250,000 deaths every year from cellphone-distracted driving.

Going back to the advent of cellphones, when the rest of us harshly judged those who deemed themselves worthy of a mobile device, the earliest cellphone users defended themselves with one argument. And it was actually pretty persuasive. Hell, the first kids to get them in school all used the same argument. It was like a rite of passage. Get your driver's licence, and then get a cellphone. It can be dangerous out there on the roads, the wisdom of the time said. Have a cellphone with you when you're driving; it's better to be safe than sorry.

The smartphone, much like social media, can be a force for good. What's that old saying? "Too much of a good thing." That's it, that's the whole cliché. Whoever first said it never finished their thought—I guess they got a text. Running late to meet someone because of a legitimate, out-of-your control event? Thank you, phone. Running late to meet someone because you were on your smartphone uninterrupted for more than an hour yet somehow didn't notice or care about the time being displayed directly in front of your eyes because you can always text the person that you're ten minutes away when you're twenty minutes away in an Uber you didn't actually need? Fuck you, phone.

Point being, smartphones present opportunities and challenges at the same time. If you have a loved one who lives in another country, communicating with them is as simple as reaching into your pocket. That's what the purpose of the phone is supposed to be: to connect us. The funny thing is I've seen my phone disconnect me more than anything. My severe trust issues make me wary of every single new person I meet. When I have my phone, I don't have to face those issues; I just have to face a screen. On the mornings when I wake up with my sheets drenched in sweat from night terrors, I can stay in bed all day, not doing anything but scrolling on my phone. I know it won't make me feel better, but it distracts me and numbs the pain—or worse, helps me find somewhere to direct that anger. After a bout of depression, I always notice my right arm and neck are sore. It's from holding my phone and looking down for so long.

Are smartphones addictive on a physiological level? It's not officially accepted as a clinical addiction, yet. However, when I think back to the statistics from social media use from the previous chapter, I just wonder. If humans spent 1.9 trillion hours on social media alone in 2019, how long did we spend on our smartphones in general?

At quitting time, I thought about buying a flip phone to replace my smartphone, but I didn't want to be wasteful. Electronics use a lot of resources, and I felt selfish getting an entirely new one while I had a perfectly functional one already. Technically, I may have still had a smartphone, but I deleted all the apps. The only thing it could do was text and make calls.

• • •

There were 14,000 people in Barclays Center in Brooklyn that night. You already know how me and Denzel Washington (not seated together because of an unforeseen scheduling error) got here, so I'll tell you how three other people did.

Luis Ortiz got here by leaving his homeland in Cuba on a small boat, and then by walking across the Mexican desert, with one shoe. He had his first professional fight in America one year later, in two shoes. He fights southpaw and for his daughter, Lismercedes. She has a skin condition called epidermolysis bullosa, and it is painful, to say the least. She has only one layer of skin, so even the slightest friction can induce third-degree burns. By this fight, Ortiz was undefeated and looking to become the first ever Cuban heavyweight champion of the world.

To do that he'd have to beat Deontay Wilder, who got here by way of Alabama, where he first walked into a boxing gym at nineteen after dropping out of college. He has one of the most unconventional styles ever seen and does all the things trainers tell a new boxer not to do on day one. Going against all traditional boxing wisdom, he won a bronze medal in the Olympics. Wilder fights orthodox and for his daughter, Naieya. She was born with spina bifida. It's why her father dropped out of college and walked into a boxing gym. By this fight, Wilder was the undefeated heavyweight champion of the world.

Nora got here by using her mom's Air Miles. But considering everything she'd been through over the last year, that was the only uninspiring part of her journey. Oddsmakers would tell you not to defect from your authoritarian country, and then cross an ocean and a desert wearing only one shoe. Oddsmakers would also tell you not to drop out of college and try to become a boxer without any experience. Oddsmakers would definitely tell you not to date another addict so early in both your sobriety journeys. Oddsmakers would have bet against the four of us making it to that evening.

No crowd dresses like a boxing crowd. That night, I saw women in mink coats clutching Louis V bags, wearing eight-inch heels and twenty-four-carat diamonds. I saw men with sunglasses on indoors and chains worth more than the house I grew up in. The most memorable outfit of all festooned the older Cuban man sitting in the row in front of us: an orange velour track suit with several Angry Birds characters and logos all over it. This man let our entire section know that tonight we would see the first Cuban heavyweight champ crowned. He was the most frightening person I've ever seen wear the colour orange, the material velour, and the brand Angry Birds.

"The champ is here, Brooklyn!" Lil' Kim said before she rapped Deontay Wilder to the ring, where Luis Ortiz was waiting for him.

Minutes later, the six-seven, 214-pound champion was staring into the eyes of the six-four, 241-pound challenger, while a five-eight man wearing a bow tie told them both he would break them up if necessary. Hands were taped, gloves were on, robes were off, mouth guards were in, the crowd was going nuts, and then the bell rang. The first few rounds were pretty standard for a heavyweight fight, both guys respecting each other's power, and at times it resembled an intense staring contest more than a fist fight. Each guy landed a few decent punches, but things didn't heat up until the first knockdown.

At the end of the fifth round, Ortiz had Wilder trapped in the corner. Ortiz's corner yelled for him to "Let your hands go!" but their man wasn't the one who obliged. Wilder fired a right hand that backed Ortiz up and allowed him to escape from the corner. But that's the thing about Deontay Wilder—when he lands a decent punch, he isn't usually satisfied with just the one. Fifteen seconds and two Wilder straight rights later, Ortiz was down for the first time in his career.

The hardest part about picking yourself up when you get knocked down is knowing what is waiting for you once you stand up. It's not a rainbow with a marching band and a chorus line holding up a banner that reads, *Congratulations! You Got Up When You Were Down!* No, it's the same shit that knocked you down before, but now you know it can knock you down, and you know it knows it can knock you down. Times like these, it's easier to just stay down. But Luis Ortiz didn't get here by doing what's easier, so he was up before the count of five, just before the bell rang.

The sixth round saw Ortiz take a few punches you'd expect to end the fight, but every time, he threw one right back to keep the champ at bay. With a minute and ten seconds left in the seventh is where I will throw it over to Mauro Ranallo and Al Bernstein, who were doing commentary for the fight.

Assessing how the fight started going sideways for Ortiz, Al asserted, "Ortiz hasn't gotten leverage on his left hand in this fight, and he's never gotten on the inside, which is what I still feel he should be doing."

"He needs to navigate a minefield of power," Mauro agreed.

But things can change fast in boxing. Less than thirty seconds later, Mauro was screaming into his headset, "A right hook by Ortiz has Wilder in trouble. Wilder needs to hold on. He's on inline skates momentarily as Ortiz lands the hooks ... Oh, straight left hand. Wilder gets clipped ... Deontay Wilder in trouble."

That was what everyone at home was hearing. I was hearing a stadium full of people screaming, none louder than Angry Birds Man. He was on his feet, wildly throwing punches, mimicking his fellow countryman in the ring. Wilder was getting rocked repeatedly; it looked like he was out on his feet and the ref was just waiting to end the fight. Wilder was still taking shots when the ref stepped between the two men to end the onslaught.

Angry Birds threw his arms around his friend in celebration. They were yelling in Spanish, and I distinctly hear the word "*revolución*." My section had just quieted from an "overthrow the government" level of loud when someone yelled out the word "stools." That's when we all noticed the corners had put the stools down and both men were walking towards them. It was so loud we all missed the bell. That wasn't the ref stopping the fight; it was just the end of the round. Wilder had miraculously survived.

Wilder had dominated the division until tonight. He was 40–0 with thirty-nine knockouts, but a lot of people in boxing wanted him to fail to prove that you have to do things the way they say in order to win. With only three rounds to go, he was down on the cards, and it looked like all his critics were right. But Wilder didn't get here by listening to critics, and with two minutes left in the tenth round, he landed a big straight right that hurt Ortiz.

Now Angry Birds had his arms up in a guard and he was moving his head like he was trying to dodge Wilder's fury. It didn't work, and enough straight rights hit home to send Ortiz to the canvas. The Angry Bird made a beeline for the exit, but as the Cuban velour-enthusiast passed me I said, "Look, he's getting up."

He just smiled at me and said, "No, it's finished" and walked out without looking back.

The wise man in the unwise track suit was right: Ortiz was up at the count of nine but down again soon after. This time, the ref waved the fight finished, and we had a still-undefeated heavyweight champion of the world.

Through it all, I didn't miss my smartphone for a second.

• • •

My skin is blood-red and leathery from the sun. I've been lost at sea, floating on this life raft, for weeks. An airplane in the distance might as well be a mirage, for all the good it can do me. I don't even show up as a dot from up there. Still, I have to try. I'm weak from lack of food and water, but I rise to my feet. The last breath in my body leaves my mouth in the form of a scream of one single word: "Help!" No one hears the last thing I'll ever say, and I fall to my knees. My eyes are shutting now. I wonder if they'll even know I was ever alive.

All right, I'm being a bit dramatic, but that's how cut off from the world I felt at times that first week off my smartphone when I got home. When the magic of New York was replaced by the monotony of everyday life, I really began to see the hold my smartphone had on me. I started to notice the times I would have the impulse to check my phone. It was anytime my brain wasn't already being stimulated.

By the fourth day, I did something drastic. I bought, and even read, a book. I repeated this feat the following day. By the end of my second week off my smartphone, I had read more books than I had the entire previous year. I started my day as soon as my eyes opened, instead of after my phone opened. I was sleeping, listening, engaging, and feeling better almost immediately. When I did feel the impulse to check my phone I would—you guessed it—play the tape out. The end of the tape always involved me either wasting hours at a time on the couch staring into the void in my hand, or worse, coming across some news story or troll comment that would ruin my day before it had even started.

Of everything, my smartphone was the easiest and one of the most instantaneously beneficial vice to toss from my life. However, I must also submit other variables that could have contributed to me feeling physically and emotionally better than I ever had: everything else I had quit.

Also, Nora and I moved in together. And the tremors, falling, and other symptoms had stopped for longer than they had since I'd first started experiencing them. It was like they were evil spirits exorcised from my body. Finally, I was ready to meet the man who would train me for my fight. I was sure he'd be a wise sage who'd have advice for me in and out of the ring.

"Everything is shit. You have decent cardio, but everything else is shit," said the most Polish accent I'd ever heard after watching me shadowbox in the ring for ten minutes.

Mario was a national Canadian lightweight champion and a former sparring partner of all-time great Floyd Mayweather Jr. He would remind you if you ever forgot it, and he also thought you forgot it a lot.

After my unimpressive display in the ring, I got on the heavy bag while he held on to the other side. He asked for twenty jabs.

Jab hits the bag.

"Shit."

Jab hits the bag.

"Shit."

Jab hits the bag.

"Shit."

And so on.

Then he asked for twenty straight rights.

Right hits the bag.

"Shit."

Right hits the bag.

"Shit."

Right hits the bag.

"Shit."

And so on.

Then twenty left hooks.

Left hook hits the bag.

"Shit."

Left hook hits the bag.

"Shit."

Left hook hits the bag.

Pause.

"Do that again."

Left hook hits the bag.

"Shit. Do it again."

Left hook hits the bag.

"Shit. Do it again."

Left hook hits the bag.

Pause.

"Okay, we got something."

Mario diagnosed me absolutely perfectly after this workout/ assessment.

"Why the fuck are you trying to fight like Ali? Do you think you're Muhammad Ali?"

I didn't say anything.

"You're not Muhammad Ali."

I'd always suspected it, but that didn't make the confirmation any less painful.

I had been keeping my hands low, flicking my jab, and dancing my way through the thousands of rounds on the bag and in classes, emulating my hero. As it turned out, those are bad habits when you aren't the fastest pound-for-pound fighter in history. Since I'm, like, top ten, at best, I had better start keeping my hands up.

Mario called me "shit," "slow," and several Polish words I was pretty sure were also derogatory. But the last thing he called me before I left the gym filled my heart with bliss.

"Okay, see ya Monday, champ."

I thought you had to be a champion for someone to call you champ. He must have seen something in me. No way he just threw that word around.

The next class he called several other people champ, too. This whole time I didn't know all you had to do to be a champion was show up.

● ● ●

"I haven't been following hockey much this season. Is Montreal doing well?" I asked every person I saw wearing a Canadiens jersey.

"They're terrible. They can't even—" the person always stopped when they saw the grin on my face, revealing I already knew the answer to my own question.

It was Saturday night, St. Patrick's Day, Leafs versus Canadiens in Toronto, and I was at the game alone. If you were to design a video game level meant to make me relapse on any of the stuff I had quit, this would be it, but I wasn't scared, not in the least. There were only two weeks until the end of my podcast, and of this little experiment. I was way up on all the judges' cards, and it would take a totally unexpected knockout to beat me at this point.

In the concourse, I was now screaming my question for all to hear. The Leafs fans were back-slapping me, and even some of the Canadiens fans were laughing. I was making new friends, and a couple people even offered to buy me a drink. I loved the look of confusion on someone's face when I was incorrigibly happy and obnoxiously loud, and then they found out I was sober. I was the life of section 319, and I didn't need booze to get me there. I felt like I had reached an even further height in my sobriety than I'd ever expected. There really was nothing I needed that shit for anymore.

And then I got a text that said, *Mike MacDonald died.*

I'd never had an emotional swing that big that fast. I was reeling. Even though we didn't know each other for most of it, I'd had a twenty-year relationship with Mike. For a while, every time I saw him, I'd expected it to be the last. Now he'd died when I'd least expected it. I guess comedians will do just about anything to get out of being on a podcast. I could never believe it when he came into my life, and now I couldn't believe that he'd left it.

I also couldn't believe I was in line to buy a drink.

They'd said my uncle was going to be okay, and he wasn't.

They'd said Mike was going to be okay, and he wasn't.

They're telling me that I'm okay, and I'm not.

Playing the tape out? Didn't work. No mantras or awareness of thoughts was going to pull me out of this one. Telling myself this was the last thing Mike would have wanted for me? Nope. Thinking of my friends, family, and podcast listeners who would be let down? Sorry to say it, but I didn't care about them in that moment.

Fuck it was playing in my mind on repeat, and there was no turning it down.

But I didn't get a drink that night.

What made me not do it?

Discipline.

I just got out of the line and went to my seat. No profound reason or inspiring epiphany. I just didn't do it. That's what discipline looks like. It's boring. It's not inspiring or romantic; it's robotic. There weren't even positive thoughts running through my head. I just didn't do it.

Less than two weeks later, I recorded the last episode of my podcast with no guest, just me. The clock crossed midnight while I was recording, signifying that I had gone the distance.

I had quit everything.

Almost everything.

epilogue

the fight of my life

I don't know what to compare training for a fight to. Usually, when people do something hard, they compare it to training for a fight. Actually, you know what? I do know something that hard. Training for a fight is like getting sober. The progress comes slow, and the pain comes fast.

The first time I sparred, I got lit up like a wet cigarette. "How do you light a wet cigarette?" you may ask. Repeatedly, that's how. I didn't land a single punch and got touched anytime the other guy felt like it, and he was a touchy guy. On the subway ride home I had a fresh black eye, a sore body, and a broken will.

The next time I sparred, I got dropped with a shot to the ribs by a guy almost half my size. After that, I got outboxed by a guy almost twice my age. Like earlier in my life, things were getting grimmer and dimmer with every shot I took.

But all my sparring partners had been boxing ten times longer than me—my real test would be when I was matched up with the other guy in training camp who also hadn't fought before. "No more. That's it. I'm done."

258 Float like a Butterfly, Drink Mint Tea

When you get dropped for the second time in only the first round of sparring, maybe it's best to throw in the towel.

I wouldn't know. I was the one standing.

The last training session before my fight, Mario had some final words of encouragement for me. "You can take a punch better than some pro boxers I know, and that left hook is a truck," he said, before warning me, "But if you try and box this guy, I don't know what's going to happen."

I knew that was trainer speak for me losing.

"You're going to have to bite down on your mouth guard and make this a fucking fight."

My opponent was tall and had great legs, a gas tank as good as mine, and a long straight jab. He was superior to me as a boxer in every way except one: I hit harder. We knew he was going to try to stick and move all fight and not let this thing turn into a brawl. I would have to walk him down and avoid that slick jab to get inside and find a way to unload my left hook.

It makes me so sick to say, I can barely type it: He would be the one fighting like Ali. I would be fighting like Frazier.

• • •

It's the day before my fight. I'm supposed to rest, but there's one more thing I have to do before I'm ready. I tie up my shoes, put on my headphones, and begin my run when I hear the instantly recognizable trumpets from the most famous boxing song of all time. It's beyond cliché at this point, but I am a complete sucker for the Rocky theme. And unlike with the Springsteen song, they really can't touch me here on copyright: Duhn-dunna-dun dunna-dun dunna-dun Duhn-duhn-dunna-dun dunna-dun dunna-dun Duhn-dunna-dun-da-nun-da-nun Da-duhhhhhhnn ...

The downtown Toronto skyline is the only thing eclipsing the rising morning sun as I run towards it and throw some crisp one-twos. I run past the after-hours place I used to do drugs in. The faces of the people I've loved and lost, and the ones who are still here, pass through my mind. I think of Nora and the strength she gives me. I think of all the times I failed and kept trying.

The voice of Liev Schreiber, the narrator of HBO's 24/7 boxing documentaries, is in my head.

Every fighter knows their opponent standing across the ring isn't who they are truly fighting.

I get to the base of a staircase on the edge of downtown called the Baldwin Steps. It's 110 steps adorned with trees that are just beginning to show their spring colours.

They may be technically competing against their opponent, but the real fight is within themselves.

The music begins to build to its beautiful crescendo.

My foot touches the first step. And the next step. And the next step. One step at a time, until I'm at the top, looking down at the city I was once too afraid to move to. I raise both arms in the air in victory.

The next night I lose my boxing match in a unanimous decision.

• • •

"I know we didn't get the win tonight—"

The doorbell rang, announcing the pizza had arrived and interrupting the opening line of my heartfelt speech. My family, Nora, her family, Shawn, Marito, Dylan, and Alexis were gathered at Nora's mom's house after my fight for a pizza and ice cream party. Considering dairy was one of the substances I wanted to learn to be moderate with, or at least moderate the number of times I binged on it, a pizza and ice cream party seemed like a fitting celebration for the end of the podcast *and* the fight. After we ate, I told everyone how much I loved them and thanked them for being in my corner that night and every night.

A couple weeks later, Nora and I moved into our new place, a basement apartment that was too cold but felt like it was where I always wanted to be.

I know this would be a really good place to end my story. My happy ending. But I haven't told you about the fight of my life yet.

About a week after my fight in the ring, the swelling in my jaw went away enough that I could actually close my mouth. But the tremors and the falling came back a couple months later. And they weren't the only thing to come back. I was back to smoking weed all day every day again to try to cope. Smoking weed 24/7 always feels wrong, so I satisfied some of the cravings with cigars. All the smoking left me groggy and foggy and wanting a coffee. I also ate copious amounts of red meat and dairy from takeout places for weeks at a time. I gained twenty-five pounds, and I felt like giving up.

Thankfully, Nora and her parents wouldn't give up on getting me a diagnosis, and with their help, I got an appointment at the Centre for Movement Disorders. After some tests I was diagnosed with functional neurological disorder. The way the doctors explained it to me was that the hardware in my brain was fine, but the software was broken. The tremors, night sweats, and falling were all involuntary movements but not a result of structural damage to the brain. One of the most successful treatments for FND has proven to be psychotherapy.

I never thought I could be more nervous for something than I was for the walk to the ring the night of my fight, even with Miley Cyrus's "Party in the USA" blaring. But I was wrong. The walk to the psychiatrist's office was terror in its purest form and the most scared I've ever been. I was put into group therapy with other people who had been diagnosed with FND. I felt like I was back in elementary school, in the group for troubled kids I got put into when I was in grade four. My entire body was tense. I was on the verge of screaming at the top of my lungs the entire session, but I didn't say a word.

But during this difficult time, something amazing happened. The Toronto Raptors got hot. My friends and I were at game seven when Kawhi Leonard hit the rim four times before the ball fell through the hoop to win the game as the buzzer sounded. I was there for the double-overtime game when the Raptors were down 0–2 in the Eastern Conference finals and pulled out a win to keep the series alive. And I was there for game six of that same series, when they clinched the finals and downtown Toronto turned into one big party with people dancing on top of buses. I was watching the game with Nora and my best friends, a lot of whom you've met already, when the team that was never supposed to even be there won the NBA championship.

So I would go to therapy during the day and bawl my eyes out and dry heave while the tremors attacked my body, but then I'd go to the basketball court and escape. I got to witness the most amazing moments in person, and it was such a magical run for me and the team, that I almost rewrote this book to be *Kyle Lowry and Mint Tea*, just two weeks before my deadline. I've been a Raptors fan since I was a kid, but to be honest with you, I'm not a day-one fan. They played their first game in November 1995, and I don't remember very much of that year. The only thing I do remember from that year is, during the fall, being sexually abused by a priest when I was eight years old.

For so long, I tried to do what all fighters do: pretend I wasn't hurt. But I can't do that anymore. As I type this, my palms are sweating, I'm nauseated, my throat is trembling, and I have to take deep breaths in through my nose and out through my mouth to remind myself it's not happening all over again.

Addicts can keep a secret, and I kept that one buried deep inside of me for twenty-four years.

Believe me, this is not the twist ending I wanted this book to have. Personally, I would have preferred the root cause of my physical symptoms was any one of the following reasons:

- Sports scientists would discover it was the late development of my world-class fast twitch muscle fibres that would serve me well in my new career as starting goalie for the eventual ten-time defending Stanley Cup champions: the Toronto Maple Leafs.

- My symptoms were a result of the radiation serum that was administered to me in a secret government experiment that would lead to the onset of powers not unlike those of a superhero.
- The doctors would tell me that the weight, both literal and figurative, of my enormous penis was too much to withstand and my body could no longer take it.
- I don't know if you've seen the film *Teen Wolf*, but something along those lines with similar basketball prowess but less body hair.
- The twitching and tremors were a sort of beyond-the-grave Morse code, and the ghost of John Lennon was using my body to transcribe his posthumous songwriting.
- The soul of the only undefeated heavyweight champion of all time, Rocky Marciano, was reincarnated inside me and would eventually rise to the surface, leading me to be the oldest person to ever win their first world title.

However, I'm sorry to say it's none of those reasons. I tried my best to drink, smoke, snort, eat, and even punch my way out of what happened to me. Those may have worked for fleeting moments, but they weren't what allowed me to begin to truly heal. It was therapy. The boxing, the mint tea, the quitting everything just helped me get there. At the time of this writing in 2020, it's been less than a year since I finally said I was abused out loud. I've been diagnosed with PTSD, and that is the fight of my life.

I wish this book ended with me telling you that I'm winning the fight, but I'm not. Nora and I broke up a few months ago. I told you how many times I was able to get through kicking drugs by telling myself, "This isn't forever." Now I have to figure out how to move on from something else I thought was forever.

I do have some good news.

Remember that set for Kevin Hart's LOL that I recorded at Just for Laughs that I thought was a massive failure? Maybe I was wrong, because they aired it on their season premiere, and it was one of only a handful of segments from the festival to be shown on US TV as well as their streaming platform. I'm back down to my fighting weight, and I share my bed every night with someone who makes me feel safe. Otis is a twenty-three-pound rescue from a dog meat factory in Korea. He looks like a little fox and I can't walk two city blocks without getting stopped because he is a stunner. I've had cars pull over to ask about him. My dog is so cute he stops traffic. This is the part where, in great detail, I'm supposed to draw parallels between the pain both of us have suffered in our past and how we are taking things one day at a time, together. But instead I will take this opportunity to pitch to any television producers who maybe reading our buddy cop TV show called *Paw and Order*. I'm the surly, by-the-book veteran, and Otis is my hot-shot rookie partner who won't stop hunting criminals unless it's to lick his own genitals. We are asking for $100 million per episode and Otis has full creative control.

The therapy is working, too. After weekly sessions for the last eighteen months, my physical symptoms of FND have all but disappeared. Neurologists are learning more about FND every day, and I wouldn't speculate on anyone else's experiences with it, but I know that for me therapy was the medical treatment I needed for it. Same goes for addiction.

In one of my most helpful sessions I told my therapist, Lindsay, that I've always felt stuck as a kid, that no matter what I do, I can't grow up. "Picture a fourteen-year-old pretending they're living an adult life," I said. "Trying to earn a living, paying bills, rent, relationships, turmoil, travelling around the country for work. I can't fucking do it. I'm scared all the time."

I started screaming as tears rushed from my eyes.

"Sometimes I can't even fucking go to sleep at night because I'm afraid. How am I supposed to live the rest of my life like this? What kind of adult is scared of the dark? Do you know what that's like? I can't do it anymore."

I covered my face with my hands and softly whimpered, "I can't. I can't. I can't."

It took me a few minutes to regain my composure. After my eyes dried, I drank some water and took some deep breaths. Just getting it out made me feel better. And then Lindsay asked me a question that changed my life.

"Don't you think you're doing pretty good for a fourteen-year-old?"

I do think I'm doing pretty good for a fourteen-year-old. I haven't relapsed on the most important things I quit. I'm on day 2,083 off cocaine, day 1,775 off alcohol, day 1,368 off all hard drugs, and day 1,215 off cigarettes. I had to look up the numbers because I don't need to count the days like that anymore.

I've also had the discipline and dedication to abstain from everything else on the list. Yes, I am a paragon of self-restraint, and that's that.

Jesus Christ, I have to keep this trash honesty policy even this late into the book? Fine. I'm off coffee right now, not least because I was chugging six cups a day on an empty stomach until my ulcers came back. I don't use my credit card unless I must, but sometimes I must have a shirt or food delivered to me. I seldom eat red meat and I'll go months without dairy. But then I crack and order a pepperoni, bacon, and sausage pizza, and the following morning a new me rises like a phoenix from my own fiery tears that were shed while sitting in agony on the toilet. It's a similar thing with sugar binges. I try to stop myself from needless gossiping when I recognize I'm doing it, unlike a certain friend of mine, but I'll tell you all about it some other time. My smartphone and social media use are as out of control as they've ever been. I didn't realize how bad it was until the first draft of this book was mostly emojis and 9/11 conspiracy theories. I bite my nails until they hurt, which makes it tough to type the pornographic websites I frequent near daily. I'm also currently entangled in a cycle of going months off weed, followed by months on it. I'm not giving up just yet on this whole change thing, though, and if you'd like to hear more about it, I've started doing my podcast again.

Not relapsing on booze or hard drugs and writing a book about hope and perseverance while learning how to navigate PTSD and losing the person I expected to spend the rest of my life with—all during lockdown for a global pandemic—hasn't been easy.

Faith is something I was taught from a young age. They were right when they told me that I needed to have it. They were just wrong about where I should put that faith. I have faith in myself. I will make it through this. *We* will make it through this.

It's a struggle for me, but I have faith in people. For a long time I didn't. That's because I was doing the addict thing where I was looking at only the bad. It's easy for me to doubt the goodness in humanity, but I know it exists. I only have to read the names of the people in this very book for proof of that.

I tried to avoid saying anything directly to addicts while writing this book. I didn't want it to be a how-to manual, because I'm still trying to figure out exactly how to. However, I have to say this to anyone who's suffering with addiction right now. I don't know anyone who stuck with sobriety whose life didn't get better. You could be in withdrawal, planning your suicide for April 1, and then one day find out that your book is coming out on that same day eleven years later.

The last thing I want to say is that I figured something out about boxing that I don't think anyone else has. I wanted so badly for this book to end with me standing triumphant in the centre of the ring, with Nora by my side. Instead, I'm down.

Since the very beginning, the wisdom of the sport has said how much harder life is than boxing. But there's a big way that life is easier. In the traditional Queensberry rules of boxing, when you're knocked down, you have until the referee's count of ten to rise to your feet, or you lose.

Life has no ten count. You're never out of the fight, no matter how long you've been down. You just have to get back up.

acknowledgments

When you write a book about how you're not dead, it feels weird to only acknowledge the people who helped you with the book thing and not the whole helping-keep-you-alive thing. For that reason, I have to thank all of my family and friends before anyone else. You kept me alive during the darkest times, and I love you all with all of my heart. I am lucky enough to say that I can't name every person individually because it would take too long, but there are five names that need to be recognized. Jim, Sandra, Kate, Zac, and Bob.

Thank you to Brian, Jaz, Shirarose, and everyone at Arsenal Pulp Press and Robin's Egg. A special thank-you to Charlie, without whom none of this would be possible. You gave me this opportunity and the best writing education of my life. You brought out the best in me. You'd make one hell of a boxing trainer.

I am obligated to mention the lifetime debt I owe to Kyle Lowry and the Toronto Raptors. Just when I was feeling all of the worst things from when I was a kid, you made me feel all of the best things about it.

To all of the broken, insecure, self-obsessed children disguised as adults who call themselves comedians: thank you, you're the most fun part of my life, and no one gets me like you. Do your time.

I want everyone who supported my podcast and wrote to me to know their words have been the achievement my life.

ALEX WOOD is a comedian, writer, and podcaster who has been featured on NBC's *Today Show*, Kevin Hart's LOL, *Vice,* and SiriusXM Radio. His podcast *Alex Wood Quits Everything*, which was nominated for a Canadian Comedy Award, takes listeners on a journey through his addiction and subsequent recovery. *Float like a Butterfly, Drink Mint Tea* is his first book.

Float like a Butterfly, Drink Mint Tea is the latest
title to be published under the Robin's Egg Books imprint.
Robin's Egg Books features some of the freshest, smartest,
and, above all, funniest writing on a variety of culturally
relevant subjects. Titles in the imprint are curated and edited
by comedian, playwright, and author Charles Demers.

Previous Robin's Egg Books:

*So You're a Little Sad, So What? Nice Things to Say to Yourself
on Bad Days and Other Essays* by Alicia Tobin

*What I Think Happened: An Underresearched History of the
Western World* by Evany Rosen

*You Suck, Sir: Chronicles of a High School English Teacher
and the Smartass Students Who Schooled Him* by Paul Bae